# EVELYN DUVALL'S HANDBOOK FOR PARENTS

*Evelyn Millis Duvall*

**BROADMAN PRESS**

Nashville, Tennessee

© Copyright 1974 • Broadman Press

ISBN: 0-8054-5610-4 (hardback)
ISBN: 0-8054-5609-0 (paperback)

4256-10 (hardback)
4256-09 (paperback)

Library of Congress Catalog Card Number: 73-85699

Dewey Decimal Classification: 649

Printed in the United States of America

# CONTENTS

# 1. PARENTS—OF COURSE YOU CARE!

"I've heard enough about parental apathy," a father recently said. He went on to report that every time he had to say no to some worthy cause in behalf of children, he was made to feel that he was letting his youngsters down.

*Parents are bombarded from every side with demands for their time* and that of their children. They are made to feel guilty if they refuse to go along with some activity that others undertake with enthusiasm. Today's parents must choose from a wide variety of possibilities for their time, energy, and resources in behalf of their families. They cannot possibly do everything that someone else thinks would be good for them. They have the responsibility to choose what they feel is right and to protect themselves and their children from unnecessary pressures from well-meaning or commercially exploitative sources.

*Unloving critics wax eloquent about parental neglect and apathy.* They cite the occasional case of parents bogged down with problems too heavy to carry, who abuse, neglect, and abandon their children. But, the happy fact is that for the one parent who doesn't care (or doesn't seem to), there are literally millions of other mothers and fathers who care deeply about their families and devote themselves wholeheartedly to the rearing of their children.

## Children Are a Major Investment

Your children represent the biggest investment you will ever make. By the time you raise your youngsters to be independent, you typically will have spent more on them than on anything else—home, car, recreation, health, or any other one aspect of your life. You do this gladly, rarely begrudging the money it costs to keep modern children properly clothed, fed, schooled, in good health, with teeth looked after and possibly straightened,

7

and psyches watched so that they too grow straight and tall in time.

*Your emotional investment in your children is even greater* than the financial costs of rearing a child at today's prices. By the time you have watched over your sons and daughters as they struggled through learning what is right and wrong, you are apt to feel drained and spent yourselves. Just getting through the first few years of a child's life when so many hazards present themselves (in the form of accidents, children's diseases, bad influences in the community, and disrespect at home) you know the depth of the emotional commitment it takes to raise a family. By the time your children are in the second decade of life, your worries really begin as you, and they, are faced with the dangers of highway crack-ups, sex-jams, drug-usage, and all the other hyphenated dangers that pepper the teen years today.

*You still remain their parents after your children are grown* and gone. You are on hand when they need you, to help when you can, and to go through it all again with your grandchildren. This you do happily, generously, glad to be able to help your young adult children with a down payment on the first car, their first home, or the first baby. You continue the devotion that most parents give their children as long as you live.

### Parent-Power

Your generation saw the discovery and unlocking of the power at the heart of the atom. You have witnessed the first attempts to explore outer space. You have been a part of the technological revolution that has relieved mankind of the drudgery that bowed men's backs through the centuries.

*The potential still to be released in the soul of man* is greater than the unleashed power in the physical universe. Of urgent need right now is the exploration of inner space, within the spirit of each of us, that will match man's flights into outer space. Thrilling as space flights are, they have not the promise for the future that parent-power is capable of. Why? Because it is good people who are the world's greatest need. And, good people are the products of good upbringing, the expression of parent-power in action.

*Parents produce the persons who make life what it is* in any generation. The way in which parents are bringing up their children right now will determine more than anything else the shape and caliber and nature of the future of mankind. Others contribute to a child's well-being, welfare, and education, but all others' influence is funneled through parents.

Schools provide educational opportunities, teaching staff, materials, and programs, but it is parents who motivate their children to learn, or to resist what the school has to offer.

Churches, Sunday Schools and a wide variety of religious agencies stand officially for the religious education of children and the spiritual life of its people. But all must recognize that a child's religious life is shaped not only by the hour or more he spends in church on Sunday, but also by what happens in his home through the rest of the week—in every hour of his interaction with his parents who translate the teachings of their faith into action within the family.

Teachers, doctors, ministers, and neighbors come and go throughout a child's life, but his parents remain to the end of his days as the most important influence on his personality, his stance toward life, and the kind of person he becomes.

## What the World Needs Today

The greatest need of the world today is the kind of person who can survive and thrive and make a creative contribution to his community. Such a person is not necessarily the hardworking, thrifty, somber character symbolized by our Puritan fathers, who had to be tough to survive the harsh realities of their period. The kind of personality needed today is not so much a doer, as a becomer. His life is measured not only by the quantity of his production, or the amount of money he makes, but by the quality of life he embodies.

*The most-needed personality qualities today* have certain built-in specifications that have emerged as essential by specialists in human development and societal well-being. Some of these qualities are:

(1) Ability to love others, seen and unseen, as oneself;
(2) Willingness to live with difference;
(3) Inner peace that can wait for satisfaction;
(4) Competence to make rational decisions, with increasing integrity;
(5) Eagerness to assume real responsibility for oneself and others;
(6) Flexibility to be truly creative in new situations;

(7) Joy of relating closely to nature and its wonders;

(8) Satisfaction of helping others find fulfillment of their potential;

(9) Excitement of curiosity and continual development of one's interests; and

(10) Reverence for life in all its forms and functions.

Such an individual has a deep respect for other persons and a diminished competitiveness and combativeness, if he is to contribute to the search for peace that must begin in the hearts of men. He uses no more than he needs of the world's wealth, so that further depletion of our natural resources may be stayed. He cares deeply for the human condition, and works with others for the improvement of man's lot wherever he is. He is profoundly religious in that he views himself as a child of God whose life testifies to God's amazing grace.

This is a tall order for modern parents. The more alert a mother and father are to the needs of their children on the one hand and the requirements of their society for them on the other, the more humble they are in their task as parents. Fortunately they have a great deal going for them in their roles as parents today. One of the most powerful forces working for parents is the love they share and generate.

## You Care for Your Children

You care *for* your children; and you care *about* them. The two kinds of caring go together. You can't have one without the other; and this double kind of caring is uniquely parents' expression of love for their children.

Caring for your children begins with your first baby's birth, or even before as you prepare for his coming. He is completely dependent upon you for everything he needs during the first weeks and months of his life. As the nurturing adults in charge, you find his need for you demanding of your time and attention twenty-four hours a day, seven days a week. Even when you arrange for respites from your baby from time to time, your caring goes on in your continuing concern for his well-being.

As you take care of your children through the years of their growing up, you become deeply attached to them with an intense and all-encompassing love that overshadows most other loves of your life. This is universal in the care of all dependent beings. Families who raise a puppy or a kitten become emotionally attached to it so that it actually seems like a real member of the family.

There is a one-to-one relationship between caring *for* another living thing and caring *about* it. If this be true of animals, how much more parents love their children, whom they see as their own flesh and blood. It is this atmosphere of love that rounds out parents' development as adults. Quite as essential is its emotional warmth which children need for their fullest development.

*Children need your care to thrive.* Research and clinical evidence back your parental conviction that love is an essential for healthy development. Neglected, unloved babies lose interest in life, and turn from other persons as sources of comfort. Only the child who feels loved and cared for, has a solid basis for his further growth as a person.

### Caring How Your Children Feel About You

Your investment of yourself in your children means that you care about how they feel about you. You want them to return your love, in ways beyond their ability at times. You warm to their affection and may become demanding of them for it.

In your search for your child's devotion, you may be too eager to please. There are parents who so fear risking the loss of their children's love that they fail to provide the limits every child needs from his parents. Some parents try to be pals of their children, rather than the mature guiding adults their youngsters need, in the vain hope of being more adored as peers than as parents. Being too eager to please your children can be a mistake—for them and for you.

Is appreciation too much to expect, you ask. The simple reply is no of course not, as long as it is not demanded unduly. Children normally respond with affection and appreciation to the loving care they receive. The occasionally ungrateful child is sometimes one of whom too much overt thankfulness is demanded, rather than encouraged. Parents who set the example of expressing appreciation for what they receive, model for their children ways of putting gratitude into action.

### Carrying on the Family Tradition

Parents usually want to have their children be a credit to the family. By which they mean, carry out the family heritage and conform essentially to family expectations. Interestingly, this is the overwhelming tendency in most families. Children tend to do what is expected of them if they can. They usually identify with their parents, and from early childhood follow in their parents' footsteps. Thus, most children, in most respects reproduce the family patterns and carry on the family traditions.

There is another way in which children react to what their parents are, not by modeling themselves after them, but by doing exactly the opposite as far as they can. An example is the child brought up by alcoholic parents, who sees the heavy price his folks pay for their indulgence, and who responds by becoming a teetotaler himself. Or, we all have known children whose parents were so rigid in their religious training that by the time the children became teenagers, they had become alienated from the church and their parents' religious orientation.

*Whether a child reproduces or repudiates his family patterns* is not a matter of chance. Apparently it depends upon how satisfying he has found his life with his parents, especially in his formative years. If his parents' way of life has brought him satisfaction and fulfillment, if he has admired his family and felt a part of it, he tends overwhelmingly to carry on the ways of living he has learned to enjoy.

But when a child's experience with his parents has brought him more pain than pleasure, more sorrow than satisfaction, he may tend in his distress to turn from the ways of his parents into quite different life-styles. Having a child rebel from them and their way of life is not easy for parents to accept. It is hard to understand when one or more of the other children may be identifying comfortably with them. The explanation for such variation lies in the difference among children in the same family. What one child finds satisfying another may feel is stultifying. What enhances one child's development may be less beneficial to his brother or sister. This is one of the great challenges of parenthood—to attempt to meet each child's need in the uniquely satisfying ways that mean most to him at his stage of development.

## Sometimes You Care Too Much

Caring for your children is the best thing you can do for them. But it is possible to care too much. You can do them more harm than good with the wrong kind of love. A good example is seen in the "smother love" that stifles a child's initiative with his mother's too close supervision and too intense affection. She cares so much for him that she cannot leave him alone to live his own life and be his own person in his own way. Fathers are sometimes known to love their daughters so much that they interefere with the girl's normal love development—from loving her father to being able to love other men in other ways.

Another form of caring too much is seen in being so involved in your child's affairs that your life is all wrapped up in his. Then, when he does something that upsets you, you are deeply hurt and feel at loss suitably to express your feelings. It is then that you overreact to what is going on in your child's life. Your composure is lost, at least temporarily, and you fly off the handle, say things that you do not mean, and make issues that do no good for your youngster, to yourself, or with your relationships.

Another manifestation of the same phenomenon occurs when you care so much and feel so strongly that you are afraid to say anything for fear of saying too much. You remain tight-lipped and uncommunicative when a few words or gestures might lessen the tension between you—if your feelings were not so violent.

This is part of the price parents pay for caring for their children. Their only safeguard from letting their love become too possessive, or too strong for expression, is in refraining from letting their children become the be-all and end-all of their lives. Important as children are in the family, they are not all their parents have to live for. They are nurtured best by love that is responsive to their needs and by caring that allows them room to grow on their own.

It is at this point that child development specialists and students of family life concur that the central relationship in the home must be the husband-wife axis and not the parent-child tie. A child cannot be expected to bear the burden of his parents' frustrations and adult hungers. It is only when husband and wife meet one another's needs in satisfying ways that they free themselves for wholesome love of their children. Such a marriage is the true heart of the home and the wellspring of caring for children in optimal ways. Even the one-parent family must find ways of safeguarding the children from the single parent's affectional needs.

This opening chapter simply lays the foundation for the rest of the book which deals with the parents' eye-view of their children. There are many volumes available on child care and rearing. There are all kinds of specialists with good advice on how to raise a family. The thing that makes this book different is that it is parent-centered. It focuses on parents' roles and feelings and frustrations in ways that hopefully will be reassuring and helpful.

*Few parents are apathetic about their children.* Most mothers and fathers care deeply about their families and try to do the best they can for them. They are bombarded with complicated and often conflicting pressures at every turn until they are made to feel too often inadequate and ineffective. It is my thesis that parents are the most important persons their children will ever know. Their influence is more profound and far more lasting than even the best-paid professional consultant or specialist can be for any particular child.

*Parents today are largely ignored* for the central roles they play in their children's lives. They lack the clout and the voice that would give them confidence in their own power. They work alone in family and neighborhood, with little group support or reassurance. They have access to far too little of the knowledge of normal child development processes that would simplify their work. They have a right to the encouragement and guidance such a book as this attempts to give.

This is not to suggest that a militant "parents' lib" movement be formed to give parents their due at long last. Few would join such a movement if it were to be started—they are far too busy doing their job to get organized!

My thesis is that I believe in parents individually and collectively. I think that parents generally are doing a tremendous job in a time in history when it is not easy to raise a family.

If more parents can find delight in living with their children, as well as the awesome responsibility of guiding their children's lives, then this book will have served its purpose. So happy reading, parents. Do talk back to the author as you read. Take nothing at face value; even if it is true generally, it may not apply to you and your family. Use this guidebook not as a road map, but as a friendly counselor who is available as a sounding board for your feelings and frustrations, your pleasure and your pain along the road you traverse as parents.

# 2. MIXED FEELINGS ARE NORMAL

How well we know children's mixed feelings! A child's mood can swing from laughter to tears and back again within a matter of minutes. A little youngster can be full of confidence one moment and clinging with fear the next. He can shift from hugs and kisses to studied avoidance of the same person for whom he had shown affection just a short time before.

*Mixed emotions begin in early infancy.* A baby can be yelling for attention in his crib one minute and bathed in happy wriggles of pleasure as soon as he sees his mother approach. If she keeps him waiting too long, he may greet her with an angry reproach rather than wreathed in smiles. He lets her know, long before he is able to talk, when he is pleased with her, and when he is annoyed. He scolds her without needing any words to express his feelings. Then, when he gets his feeding, he calms down, and is content once again.

*Children old enough to talk put these changing emotions into words.* Little youngsters have been known to cuddle affectionately to one of their parents with outspoken, "I love you, Daddy." Then at some slight frustration draw back with frowns and a shouted, "I hate you, I hate you!" toward the same parent, if the child is allowed to express himself that overtly.

*Teenagers are widely recognized for their mixed feelings,* and rapidly shifting moods. They can be so mature and poised in one situation, and then cling like children half their age in another. They can be head over heels in love one day and "could not care less" about the same person the next. Their feelings toward their parents may be even more contradictory—at times warmly confidential and at other times, with the same parent, coolly aloof and uncommunicative.

It is easy for parents to recognize these mixed feelings in their children. It helps to understand that all these emotions are normal and a part of the reactive repertoire of a growing young-ster. It is even more helpful to accept the fact that a certain amount of ambivalence is quite normal in any close relationship.

*Wherever there are intense emotional ties,* there are apt to be contradictory feelings. In relationships where one invests little of oneself, one's feelings toward another person can remain calm, and relatively stable. That is one reason why a child can be so much more courteous and uniformly pleasant outside the family, and so much more easily wrought-up and upset at home. This phenomenon baffles many a parent who openly asks, "Why is my child such a little model of good behavior in a neighbor's house and such a disagreeable youngster at home?" The answer is not too hard to find. At the neighbors, a child is on his good behavior because he doesn't belong to them, and he can leave whenever he wishes without threat. At home he has a great deal at stake. He is deeply involved with his parents and they with him. So, more emotions are generated, of every sort and of often conflicting feeling tones.

## Why Parents Are Ambivalent

Mothers and fathers have mixed feelings about their children for much the same reasons that their children have contradictory feelings about them. The emotional investment each has in the other means that both parents and children feel strongly about one another. And, because they feel strongly, there are elements of ambivalence in both the children and their parents.

*Because you care about your children,* you feel strongly about them. You can be relatively calm and unruffled with someone else's child, because he is not your responsibility. With your own youngster, your love and your caring for him brings you both more pleasure and more pain in your relationship with him.

*Sometimes your emotions are almost too much to bear.* You are frightened by the intensity of your own feelings. You love your children but sense that you must express your love sensibly without smothering them with overwhelming sentiment. You care about how your children behave, and you become upset when they do not measure up to your expectations. Then you feel so angry, with frustration about them, that sometimes your anger can reach an almost violent crescendo if you aren't careful. So, you curb your negative feelings in order to keep from expressing too much aggression. If you didn't love your children quite so much, you wouldn't get so mad at them. Actually, you have a great many feelings about your children which are perfectly normal. These varied emotions can be managed best when they are clearly understood and accepted.

## Good Feelings About Your Children

It is easy to recognize and accept the many happy feelings you have about your children. You love them dearly, and enjoy your feelings of warmth and affection toward your sons and daughters. You welcome their expressions of appreciation and love for you and encourage these warm interchanges of caring that are so much a part of your relationship as parent and child.

*You probably take pride in your children's growth.* You are proud of your baby's progress, the way he learns and develops so nicely. You look with pleasure upon your toddler's straight little back and fine sturdy legs, as well as his fast-growing ability to fend for himself in so many ways. You take your children to Sunday School with a lump of sheer pleasure in your throat. You see them off to school with pleasure and pain—pride in their accomplishments and pain at seeing them grow up and away from you so soon. And so it goes all through your life with your own children. You find deep satisfaction in them and their development, at the same time you feel the sense of loss at how much less of your ministrations they need as they grow up.

*You and your children share a common heritage,* and a similar life-style. Because they are your children, they are growing up in many ways in your way of life. The chances are that they cherish many of the things you have taught them to value. They share many of your tastes and preferences. They probably respond much as you do to many situations. You have more in common than the sharing of your home: you actually share your life with one another in ways that can be deeply satisfying.

*One definition of love is "what you have been through together."* This applies especially to members of the same family who have been through the most meaningful and significant experiences any of them will ever know, with one another. This is one basis for the "blood is thicker than water" saying. It is the primary reason why feelings in the family so often run so high and express themselves so vigorously.

Good feelings about your children give you a good feeling about yourself. You expect to love and take pleasure in your youngsters, so these emotions do not upset you. On the contrary, happy feelings about your children make you feel good. Pleasant emotions in connection with your children are comforting, reassuring, full of the confidence you need in yourself and in them. Some of the other feelings that are not so positive may be more difficult to recognize, to face, and to accept. But they are there, nevertheless.

## Unpleasant Feelings About Your Children

Unhappy feelings about your children and about your relationships with them are quite as much a part of your life as are the good feelings. The difference is that the happy feelings are easy to take, and the unpleasant emotions are hard to tolerate or even to accept as part of the picture.

*Worry and anxiety go with parenting.* If you never want to be worried about another human being, you had best not become a parent. It is not possible to bring up a child in a world full of hazards without becoming worried about him from time to time. This all starts while your child is but an infant, as you feel concerned about his health, his habits, his rate of development, his dependence upon you, or his independence of you.

As children grow, parents have even more to be anxious about. Toddlers get around the house with its pitfalls for the unprotected. You turn your back for even a minute, and little youngsters can be into the cleaning fluid, or handling a knife, or playing with fire. They get out into the yard where many accidents occur. You can't watch them every minute, especially when they are out into the neighborhood or at school, where all sorts of unsavory experiences are possible.

You rightly worry about the frightening aspects of the drug traffic that in some communities reaches down into the grade-school level. You shudder at the dirty pictures and materials that turn up among supposedly nice kids. You fear the sexually disturbed child-molester, the abductor, and the exploitative adult who can so scar your youngster in a brief encounter.

In the meantime, you are bandaging your son's badly cut hand or rushing him home from the neighborhood ball park with a bump on his head. At some time or other, you know what it means to sit up all night with a sick child, wondering in your anxiety whether he will make it and what you could have done to protect him from this hazard.

*Guilty feelings about your shortcomings as parents* are almost inevitable at times. You cannot be everything for your child. You cannot do everything for your youngsters. While you are paying attention to one thing that they need, something else goes undone. Then, when something unfortunate happens, you blame yourself. You convince yourself that if you had been more diligent, your children could have been spared some painful experience that has befallen one or more of them.

*You know that feeling guilty does little or no good.* It but undermines your own feelings of self-confidence and may weaken a bit your youngster's sense of security with you. But feeling guilty is not a rational matter. Like the other feelings parents have from time to time, it is irrational, subjective, and is there whether you want to feel that way or not.

*Being annoyed with your children can be exasperating.* You are understandably upset with something the youngsters have done, and you compound the problem by losing your own self-control when you and they need it most. You find yourself yelling at the kids, or scolding them, even while you know that your shouting or nagging is no doubt doing more harm than good. Your annoyance that started with your feeling about your child is compounded with chagrin about your own reaction, until your feelings become almost too much to bear.

## Mixed Feelings Are Inevitable

Everyone has mixed emotions about himself and others. At times you feel good about yourself and your children. At other times, quite as normally, you are upset and unhappy about yourself, your family, and your whole situation. Somehow these mixed feelings have to be lived with, hopefully with some insight and understanding.

Recognizing the presence of mixed feelings can be helpful. As soon as you can acknowledge the presence of your own contradictory feelings, you are better able to cope with them. One of the best ways to help a child caught in the fury of his own hatred or anger is to help him see that sometimes he feels mad and other times he feels loving. A wise parent or teacher can openly say to a child: "Right now you don't like me very much. But sometimes you do. That is the way it is."

*Acknowledging your own mixed feelings helps* both you and the others in the family. Alerting those who live with you that you are not feeling up to par on a certain morning can help you put your malaise into words. Such action can ease the feeling of responsibility your spouse and your children might otherwise have about whatever is troubling you. Openly telling your dear ones that you love them, even when you are angry or upset, can give both you and them the perspective you all need in the uneasy situation.

### You Have a Right to Your Own Honest Feelings

There is no reason why parents should expect themselves to be paragons of virtue all the time. Actually, parenthood is one of the most difficult and exacting roles a man or woman can play. It is full of emotional upheaval. Just because a man is a father is no reason to expect that he will never lose his cool and act like a little boy at times. Just because a woman is a mother is no guarantee that occasionally she will not measure up to her own definitions of what a good mother should be and do. She is going to feel like the particular individual she is in the situation in which she finds herself. Some of these occasions will be satisfying and gratifying; others just as naturally will be frustrating and annoying. Accepting this simple fact goes a long way toward easing the guilt and other negative feelings parents have about themselves.

You are wise to acknowledge that sometimes you love your children deeply; at other times, quite as naturally, you need to get away from them, at least for awhile. Sometimes you feel confident, and other times, for good and sufficient reasons, you feel inadequate and out of sorts with others and with yourself.

You have a right to your own honest feelings about your children, about your situation, and about yourself. These emotions shift and change as you, they, and the problem change. Your feelings are in a sense a barometer of the pressure you are under at the moment. Your emotional climate in the home varies quite as much as the weather, and for quite similar reasons of changing fronts, and high and low pressure areas that develop between persons in any family.

### Handling Your Emotions

You do not want to go around with your emotions all unbuttoned. You have been brought up to control your feelings, so that they will not harm others or shame you unduly. Some controls are essential for civilized living. But too much of the wrong kind of control can be harmful too. So somehow, you have to learn how to express your feelings in ways that are healthful and helpful.

*Suppressing strong feelings can take physical forms.* The man who feels that his burdens have become more than he can bear may complain of a backache. The mother who has been swallowing her own anger through a long and difficult day may go to bed with a sore throat or a touch of indigestion. Each person has his own repertoire of feelings, his own way of suppressing or expressing them, and his own tendencies to feel physically the emotions which he is experiencing.

*Expressing violent emotions can be damaging.* Too well we all know the "battered baby" syndrome in which parents in fits of strong emotion actually have beaten their children within an inch of their lives. Violent feelings unexpressed can be harmful too since they crop out unexpectedly and explosively when they are least expected. Multi-problem families are often those in which each member makes himself, and the others, sick, because of the unhealthy way in which they handle their feelings.

If repressing your feelings can be harmful and expressing your hostile impulses is too dangerous, what can you do to handle your emotions wisely? This is a basic question, that every parent must answer in his or her own way. The better you are at managing your own feelings effectively, the better parents you will be and the happier you and your family will be as individuals.

Venting hostility in safe and nonhurtful ways is a must for modern parents. Your lives are so full of both minor and major frustrations and incomplete satisfactions that ways must be found to keep them from building up into full-scale aggression. The recommended principle is to keep your feelings expressed as you go along in safe and satisfactory ways. Then they do not let you get so tense with pent-up feelings that you may "blow your top." Even a safety valve blows off when the pressure gets too big a head of steam behind it.

*There are many good ways of letting your feelings out* without hurting yourself and others. You can get rid of a great deal of tension in physical exercise—walking, swimming, sports, garlening—whatever brings you a sense of peace and release. Some musically inclined persons can pound out their feelings on a keyboard or whistle into the wind. Artists get a healthy release of both their emotions and their talent by their creations. Socially sensitive persons throw themselves into community service and get the satisfaction of doing good at the same time that they release some of the excess feeling that otherwise might spill over into their family relationships.

Disappointment and sorrow can be expressed by a good cry, by talking out your despair with a confidante you can trust, or by taking it to the Lord in prayer. Any and all of these can be effective. Each satisfies some persons' needs in demonstrable ways. Parents like all other people must learn what works for them when they are blue, bedeviled by problems too difficult to solve, or trying to manage some other unhappy feeling in ways that are truly helpful.

*Expressing love in ways that are appropriate* to the age and sex and relationship of the other person and yourself has to be learned, too. In the family most love feelings can be expressed openly and freely, to the benefit of the whole family and every one in it. But there are limits that must be remembered even at home. A mother wisely avoids excessive demonstrativeness with her teenage son whose struggle to become a man emotionally able to love others beyond his family is so intense. She takes her cue from him and becomes more casual and light-hearted in her contacts with him than may have been necessary a few months earlier. So too, a father learns new ways of letting his daughter know that he admires and loves her, as she begins to be and to feel like a young woman and no longer his little girl.

### Be Good to Yourself

Christian parents are vulnerable in their inclination to be self-sacrificing and self-effacing. You have been brought up to be unselfish, and to give yourself and your resources, your energy, and your life to others. This Christian ideal makes fine persons, *if* they manage in the process to see to it that their own fundamental needs are met along the way.

A wise family counselor says, "Give yourself permission to be human." God does not expect you to be other than the person you truly are. Aspiring to perfection is to negate the reality which is the real you. You have certain rights in the family that are worth protecting—clearly and openly when they are endangered. It does not help your children to make a doormat of you, and it can seriously damage your relationship with them, as well as your own sense of worthiness.

Being good to yourself includes keeping up at least some of your own central interests, even while your children are small. As you feel yourself growing into a more and more interesting person, you are a better parent and a happier person. It does not hurt your children to be left with a family member or other reliable sitter while you as husband and wife have a weekend away from home from time to time. The idea of a second honeymoon is a sound one, again and again through the years. Even on a daily basis, you can get away for something you really enjoy and return a better mother or father for it.

Children have a sound basis for respecting and enjoying their parents as persons when they see them in roles other than those of mother and father. They do not need a pair of slaves to care for them with no respite and few personal pleasures. They as children need most of all loving parents who care for them, but not with all their love; and who take care of them, but not with all their time.

*Keeping a family happy most of the time* is a goal worth striving for. A good family is not one bowed with responsibilities and torn with never-ending problems. There has to be gaiety and joy and fun in everyday living to make home a good place in which to spend one's life. Religious families are those alive with the radiance of the good life that shines in the faces of their members. Christian homes are places where everyone is good to everyone else, most of the time. In such an atmosphere of being good to be with, parents can relax and enjoy each other and their children. The nice thing about it is that kids thrive in such families, too!

# 3. FOUNDATIONS OF FAITH IN INFANCY

Infancy is the most important period in an individual's life. It is then that a baby develops the foundations of faith—in himself, in others, in life itself. His earliest experiences give him the feeling that he can trust his body to function well. His first handling by his parents provides a baby with confidence in other people. A baby's introduction to his world sets the tone for his future feelings about it. What happens during the first few weeks and months of a person's life lays the basis for the years that lie ahead.

Your faith in yourself as a parent develops early in your baby's life. It is then that you gain confidence in yourself and in your ability to be good parents. If you have a struggle in meeting your baby's needs, you may end up with a feeling of inadequacy that is hard to shake off.

*Your feelings about becoming parents* begin long before the baby's birth. As soon as you learn that a baby is on the way, you either are delighted or you feel less enthusiastic about becoming parents. If you have longed for a baby beforehand, learning that at last you are to become parents can be a cause for rejoicing. But, if you already feel swamped with more responsibilities than you can handle easily, the anticipation of still further calls upon your time and attention can seem like just too much.

One family expert has suggested that a couple have four possible combinations of reactions to the news that they are to become parents; (1) They are both delighted. (2) She is pleased, and he is upset by the news of a baby's coming. (3) He is thrilled, and she is less enthusiastic about becoming a parent just now. (4) Neither husband or wife really want to have a baby at this time. Still other couples accept their pregnancies without question and do the best they can in caring for their children whenever they arrive. Now that reliable birth control is so readily available to married couples, unwanted babies are less numerous than they once were.

## Preparing for Parenthood

Long before the baby's actual arrival, most couples prepare for his coming. The expectant mother goes regularly to her doctor or nearby clinic for prenatal checkups. She follows the regimen that is suggested to her as best she can, and her husband encourages her diet, exercise, and other procedures in his own way.

*Classes for expectant mothers and fathers* are offered in many communities by various health agencies and services. These help a couple know what to expect of themselves and their baby-to-be. Prenatal instruction usually includes enough about the development of the embryo and the fetus to give expectant parents some insight as to what is happening as their baby grows within the mother. This adds a great deal to the interest of many a couple and impresses them with the miracle of human growth and development, even before they can see their baby.

*Getting ready for the baby* can be simple and inexpensive, or it can be elaborate and costly. One pair of married students we knew simply dumped the contents of a dresser drawer into a pillow case, and lined the empty drawer with washable padding for their new baby's bed. They bathed the baby in the bathroom wash basin, carried him slung on their backs, and accepted his care casually and easily. Other couples remodel an entire room as a nursery and buy expensive equipment and layettes in anticipation of their baby's coming. Interestingly, the baby himself thrives as well with either kind of physical setting. It is the way he is cared for rather than the things in his home that the baby cares about.

*Preparing the older children* for the new baby happens whether you do it or not. If you say nothing about your expected baby, the older children probably will learn about what is happening and that you don't want to talk about it. If you speak openly about your plans for the new baby and about what having a brother or sister will mean (both a nuisance at times, and a blessing at others), the children are more likely to feel "in" on what is happening in the family.

*Questions about where babies come from* arise naturally when a new baby is on the way. It is then that a youngster old enough to talk will want to know where he came from, how boys and girls differ from the beginning, and how a baby gets started. Some of these questions are difficult for many a parent to answer comfortably. Fortunately there are excellent books available that answer his questions in a child's language. It is a good idea to read such a book to or with a child, look at and explain the pictures, and discuss his questions openly with him. If you need help in finding just the right book, or in answering your child's questions, do not hesitate to get it from a source you trust—your doctor, pastor, librarian, or other competent confidante.

*Help the first week or two* should be arranged in advance. When the new mother returns from the hospital with the new baby, she needs time to get her strength back, and to gain confidence in caring for the new baby. Perhaps her mother, or her husband's mother, comes to help care for the family while the mother and baby are in the hospital and after they return home. Sometimes, a household helper can be employed for this period. There are some men whose temperament and work schedule allow them to care for their growing family themselves.

## Father—Insider or Outsider?

There was a time when a father felt like a fifth wheel during his wife's pregnancy, and the baby's infancy. Such a man took the position that having a baby is a woman's job and caring for infants is the mother's role. So, he kept out of the picture as much as possible and began to relate to his son when he was big enough to take fishing, or at least was housebroken. Such a man missed most of the thrill of fatherhood, and all of the miracle of growth in a baby's early weeks and months.

Some mothers unwittingly keep their husbands out of the baby's life by insisting upon taking complete care of the baby themselves, and acting as though their husband is incapable of doing anything for the new baby. Wiser by far is the wife who encourages her husband to feel in on the process of baby-making and baby-care from the beginning. She is careful not to bore her husband with unpleasant or unnecessary details but shares with him all the facts and feelings that he wants to be a part of as much as she can. When he holds his baby in his arms, she lets him get the feel of it himself without unnecessary admonitions and advice. When he wants to help bathe the baby, she lets him do just as much as he wants to without interference. As he begins to feel confident as a father, she lets him know how pleased she is with him, and the baby. In such a family, both mother and father share the joys and responsibilities of parenthood as a team.

*Naming the baby* can be a joint undertaking. It may be that both know well in advance of the baby's coming what name will be best for a girl or a boy. They may have decided that the baby will be named for some favorite relative. They may feel strongly that the first girl should be named for her mother, or that the first boy would become Junior. Or, as likely as not, the couple begin to look for a new name for the baby that will be uniquely his. This involves name-searching with an ear for how the first name fits phonetically with the middle and last name. The couple should be aware of how the initials will look on luggage some day (Frederick Allen Tucker is a fine name, but how about the initials?). They should make sure that the probable nickname will be acceptable and that close relatives like the name they are choosing. Keeping in mind how the individual may feel about his or her name as a grown-up is a good idea in choosing the new baby's name.

## Feeding Your Baby

Feed your baby when he is hungry. Sounds so simple, doesn't it? Only the baby knows when he needs nourishment; his tummy tells him so in no uncertain terms. The newborn's stomach is small, and holds little at a single feeding. Some babies need to be fed more often than others, for a number of reasons that we need not go into now. Your baby tells you when he is hungry in the only way he can—by crying. It starts with a restless mewing when he is very little, and then builds up to a lusty howl, if the feeding is delayed. Making him wait when he is very hungry makes him angry, and it can make him feel that he has to fight for what he needs and that he is not living in a very loving, considerate world.

*Schedules are for nurses, not for babies.* In a busy hospital, it is easier for the nurses to feed all the babies at about the same time. Visit any hospital nursery and peek in through the glass, and you'll be able to see whether feeding time is but recently over. Then most of the babies are sleeping peacefully. But as the time goes on more and more of the newborns become restless, and start to cry, many because they get hungry before it is time for their next feeding.

Some parents attempt to carry out the schedule the hospital had tried to establish. And, with some babies it works just fine. But others are miserable with that particular timing. The mother may have to waken the baby when it's time for his feeding. Or, worse yet, baby wakens hungry, cries for food, and because the time has not yet arrived for his feeding, he must wait; while his mother anxiously bides her time until the clock says it's all right to feed her baby. Nonsense! The simple principle to follow is feed your baby when he tells you he is hungry. In time he will set his own schedule, as most happy babies do. Then you'll be able to predict fairly well when he'll be ready for his next feeding and plan your time accordingly.

*Breast or bottle is for you to decide.* This must be done by the second day of the baby's life. This is a critical time for such an important decision, because mother and baby are often not free to work things out for themselves. The doctor feels strongly one way or the other, and the nurses are too busy, oftentimes, to give the new mother the patient attention and encouragement she needs to get her baby started at the breast. Then, it is almost too simple to suggest that the baby get a bottle instead.

*A bottle is easier in some ways* than breast-feeding. You can tell how much the baby gets at each feeding, as is never quite so simple in breast-feeding. The bottles can be prepared ahead of time and given the baby by any convenient person. A baby may seem to prefer the bottle to the breast because the nipple can be adjusted to his sucking, and fits farther back into his mouth than does the human nipple, usually.

Many a mother chooses bottle-feeding because she knows that she is to be too much away from her baby through the first few months to be able to nurse him. An occasional husband would rather his wife not nurse their baby, because her breasts are so important in the couple's lovemaking, or because the wife will be more available to go out with him without having to get back for the baby's next feeding. These are all valid reasons for choosing bottle-feeding, all other things considered.

*Breast-feeding is preferable to bottle-feeding* for a number of important reasons. It brings the baby the food nature has prepared for him with all its good nutrients, immunization, and taste. Nursing at the breast gives the young infant more sucking time than most bottle feeding, which is important for a baby who needs to suck as well as to get food. Nursing her baby is supremely satisfying to many a young mother. She thinks of it as a culmination of the whole process of conceiving, delivering, and nurturing her baby. She feels close to her baby in a very special way that is satisfying both to the infant and to mother. As the baby nuzzles and snuggles close to her body, his hands fondle her skin, and she cuddles him close with the very special relationship that only babe and mother can share. Nursing the new baby at the breast may be threatening to the next older child of the family, who may need some special reassurance that he too is loved by his mother, as "her big boy, now."

*Bottle or breast is not a life or death matter.* Babies thrive on both methods. The important thing is that the parents feel good about whichever way they decide is right for them and then relax and feed the baby when he is hungry.

*Weaning should be at the child's pace and time.* As soon as he can hold a spoon and cup, they can be given him as playthings. As he watches others drink from a cup, he will try to when he is ready. That is the signal to put a little water, or milk in the cup and let him have his first experience in drinking rather than sucking. The doctor in whom you have your child's care will advise solid foods when he feels your baby is ready for them. Some of them the baby will enjoy, and others he will not like at all. So don't make an issue of the one he pushes away. Remove it for the time being and offer it again a few weeks later when he may like it. Most babies continue to want a bottle long after they have begun to eat solid foods. Especially at bedtime a bottle is soothing, and there is no reason why your baby should be deprived of it. When he is ready to get along without a bottle, he'll let you know. Don't let some other child's earlier weaning upset you. You are caring for *your* baby, and he is like none other that is or ever was!

### Diapers—a Big Deal?

For baby's sake and yours, don't let diapers become a big deal. Much of what goes into the baby, is going to come out in baby's own time, and way. He is not ready for toilet training for at least a couple of years, usually, and it doesn't do any good to rush him. When he is ready, and his muscles are mature enough, he will happily take to the potty chair (unless you have made an issue of it). Until that time comes, you are stuck with dirty diapers and the daily laundry.

*Change the baby when he needs it.* Unless it is cold, a baby is not uncomfortable in a wet diaper; he doesn't even mind a soiled one most of the time. When he does, he will fuss and let you know that a change is needed. Of course, you'll clean him up before letting Grandma hold him. You'll want him sweet-smelling yourself. And, you'll watch out for the telltale diaper rash that lets you know that his skin is sensitive and requires clean, dry, soothing attention.

You make changing the baby's diaper a fun time as soon as you feel comfortable about it yourself. Talk to him as you take the old diaper off, tell him what a fine body he has to be functioning so well. Pat him affectionately as you clean him up, and smile at him as you lift his legs to position the clean diaper. Then cuddle him and tell him how sweet he smells and what a good baby he is. He'll like it, and so will you.

*Bathtime can be fun for the whole family.* The baby will enjoy it as soon as you find that you can hold a slippery, wriggling baby without letting him fall. You will enjoy it when you let yourself see it as relaxing, rather than as a chore to get done. The older children in the family, and in the neighborhood, enjoy being in on the act, handing you the baby oil or powder, and helping get the tiny arms into shirt and gown. Father may ask for his turn at bathing the baby, when he gets home from work. If so, why not? Routines are made to be broken, and the father-baby tie should be encouraged for both their sakes. Talking, laughing, splashing, and water play continue to be fun for baby and the rest of the family well into the second and third year. Just be sure that baby is not left alone in the water even for a few minutes. If the phone rings, let it or bundle him up and take him with you.

## Your Baby Is Unique

From the moment conception took place, your baby has been uniquely himself, unlike any other child. His experience prenatally and since he was born has been peculiar to him alone, and different from that of all other children—even brothers and sisters in the same family.

*Where the child comes in a family makes a difference.* The oldest child arrives at a time when both his father and mother are new parents and inexperienced in caring for a baby. The first child grows up close to his parents in a way no other children do because he is the oldest and is expected to be the responsible one. The youngest child of the family is "the baby" as long as he lives, never quite catching up to the older brothers and sisters who arrived before he did. The in-between children being neither the oldest or the youngest find their own roles in the family, each in his or her own way.

One child may be the social one, making friends easily all up and down the street. Another may be musical, or mechanically inclined, or athletic, or with intellectual interests. The simple fact is that each child in the family is and must be different from all the others!

*Babies differ greatly from others of the same age.* Girls and boys respond differently from the first. Some babies are alert and vigorous, others are quiet and sleep most of the time. One baby may be sensitive to all sorts of stimuli that other babies seem to ignore. There are tense babies and others that seem from birth on to be placid and unflappable. Some infants are inquisitive, alert, and enthusiastic, while others are much more matter-of-fact. Each baby is as unique as his fingerprints, and you'd best remember it. The cardinal rule is: Accept the child you have and learn to enjoy him for the very special person that he is.

### Parents' Time Off

Taking care of a baby twenty-four hours a day, seven days a week can be a terrific strain on even the most mature father and mother. Especially if they have little help in the home (as most families used to when grandparents and assorted other relatives were readily available), a modern pair of parents occasionally need some relief from full-time baby care.

Spelling each other is a simple inexpensive way to relieve parental burdens. Nowadays it is not at all unusual to see father taking his baby with him on a shopping trip or to the neighborhood launderette, while his wife catches her breath or mops the kitchen floor! Husband and wife can alternate evenings out, for a movie or a class, or some other relaxation. This gives the baby-caring father a chance to be on his own with his baby without his wife's well-meant interference. The trouble is it keeps the parents apart.

*Parents in some neighborhoods form cooperative systems* in which they sign up as sitters for other couples, who in turn are available for them when they want an evening out. This is convenient, inexpensive, and assures you of a competent sitter when you need one. Taking care of another baby or two along with your own is not too much of a hardship, and often gives you a new pride in how nice a child you have.

Finding, training, and instructing other sitters who can spell you is well worth the effort. You learn to take advantage of time off to recharge your emotional batteries and feel that you are a person too. Nearby relatives can be enlisted as mothers' helpers sometimes. In most communities, the local home economics teacher can recommend responsible high school girls (and boys) who have shown promise in child development units or baby-sitting preparation. Older women in the church are often hungry for little ones in their lives and can be of help as they make their time and talents available to young families nearby.

*Keeping up your personal interests* while your children are small need not make you feel guilty. You will be a better mother for keeping your sense of personal identity intact, even while you are being a full-time mother. Being available to go with your husband on a trip as soon as your baby is weaned from the breast is important—to you, to him, and probably to the baby too. Taking the baby with you is possible in a good many circumstances. It provides a change of scene for you all, and unless there is sickness to be wary of, is a healthy thing to do. The older children in the family can help out, without making an issue of it. Baby will enjoy them, and they him, in time.

## Baby Development Is Fascinating

Your baby's development is a wondrous process, and you can see it all. A newborn has a big head, a small body, and tiny bowed legs. He usually is red, wrinkled, blue-eyed, and lumpy-headed. He isn't much to look at, except by his adoring parents and grandparents, but he is a bundle of tremendous potentials. He develops more in the first few months and years than he ever will again. His growth is phenomenal. If his body continued to grow at the rate he started at, he'd be a giant before he reached his teens.

By the end of your baby's first four years, he has already achieved 50 percent of his intelligence. Another 30 percent is reached by the time he is eight, and the remaining 20 percent by his seventeenth birthday. By intelligence is meant the ability to mentally handle the information he acquires. His knowledge will continue to increase as long as he keeps on learning, but the capacity to learn is established early in his life, fully half of it before he ever goes to school. His genetic potential was laid down at the moment of conception. What happens to him the first of his life determines how much of his innate capacity he is likely to develop.

*Your baby learns through his senses:* taste, sight, hearing, smell, touch, and the way he feels about what he experiences. When he mouths the nipple and sucks his thumb or a corner of his blanket, he is learning through his mouth. From the first week or two, he watches faces and follows them with his eyes. He early discovers his hands and what he can do with them. You can watch him turn his hand this way and that, as he discovers that he controls its movements. A little later, he can grab a small block with his fist, then with thumb and forefinger opposite one another on the cube. He finds that he can shake and hit and drop small objects from his crib or high chair, which delights him, so he repeats the motion over and over. Your patience may wear thin unless you can sense what is happening from his point of view and rejoice with him in his newfound ability.

*Playthings encourage your baby's learning.* While he is still flat on his back in his crib, an unbreakable mirror where he can see it will interest him. You can rig a mobile above his head that he can watch and hang a crib gym that he can manipulate as soon as he can grasp it. By this time he is ready for an infant seat, that plastic padded slant board into which he can be strapped. This will change his position, and let him watch what is going on around him.

Bathtime can be fun for all of you when you give him something to hold: a little cup, a solid rubber toy, a small swatch of terry cloth. When you bathe him in the bathroom sink, he probably can catch glimpses of you and him in the mirror that adds still another dimension to his enjoyment, and yours.

*Anything that can be looked at, handled, banged, felt, seen, or heard is a plaything* for an infant. You need very few special toys, save those doting grandparents bring. Your baby is perfectly happy with anything that gives him a new sensation and that he can manipulate himself. Let your ingenuity be your guide as soon as he can sit up and hold onto things. As long as the object is larger than a plum so that he cannot swallow it and washable so that you can keep it clean, he will find a use for it. Present him with something new to feel: a piece of washable corduroy, a clean strip of soft wool, a piece of satin, a terrycloth animal, a set of plastic spoons or measuring cups, a rubber jar ring, smooth baby blocks, and in time a large plastic jug with the top cut off into which he can drop his treasures.

*Infancy is the time for a rocking chair* in your home. Baby will like it, especially when he is restless and in need of a little cuddling. Mother may find it just the thing to nurse him in with the satisfaction both of them get in gentle rhythmic motion during and following his feeding. A little soft music from radio or record player turned low is soothing to him and his family. Little songs and lullabies have their place in his life. Sturdy cloth picture books are good from the first few months on, especially when he can "read" them as you name the objects one by one.

*Baby's own body is a source of pleasure* to him and can be to you as soon as you get over any residual hang-ups about certain body parts being "not nice." It is natural for him to explore his body. As soon as he can get his hands to his mouth, he will taste them and maybe suck his fingers or thumb if you don't make too much of a fuss about it. He'll probably be able to get his toes to his mouth in time, too. His hands will touch his genitals and the feeling will be pleasurable, until someone makes a scene about what he is doing. You can teach him that he is all right by your acceptance and encouragement of his learning about himself. Or, you can just as easily teach him by your attitude, voice, and words that he is dirty, bad, nasty, and naughty. Long before he can speak he already has learned to feel as you feel about his body, its parts, and functions, and feelings. Fortunately most parents today marvel at the wonder of life and give their babies good feelings about themselves.

### Faith Begins in Confidence

You gain confidence in your ability as a parent, in time. When you learn your strengths and weaknesses as a person, you will be a more relaxed mother or father. Then you can exercise your competence and get help for the gaps in your knowledge and skill.

*Find a doctor or neighborhood clinic* you have faith in, as soon as you can. There are bound to be unexpected illnesses, accidents, and anxieties that can be greatly relieved with professional competence. Many childhood diseases and difficulties can be avoided entirely with preventive medical attention. A bad night of croup or digestive upset can be alleviated with prompt and reassuring attention.

*Learn what to expect of children,* in general. There is a great deal of knowledge about child development that you may find helpful as parents. This does not mean that you will have a textbook baby, who is exactly as described in anyone's book. But there are certain stages of a child's development that can be anticipated, understood, and prepared for in advance. Knowing what to expect of a child of any given age is a great help in deciding your priorities as parents.

*Knowledge of critical states of child development* are of immense help in having a happy baby, and being a confident parent. This book emphasizes the most important development taking place stage by stage in a child's life. Chapter by chapter throughout this volume you will be glimpsing what is critical in your child's development at his stage of life.

*Children go through a reliable process of development* that can be understood. Each child develops at his own pace and in his own unique way, but all share the same general sequence of development. All children must learn to eat before they are ready for instruction in table manners. All children must learn to talk before they are ready to reason or to take responsibility for their conduct. All children have to be messy before they can be clean. All children have to feel good about themselves before they are self-confident.

*Your baby's basic trust in himself* lays the foundation for his faith in life. He cannot be spoiled, except by neglect and abuse, at least during his first two years. So, this is the time to do what comes naturally to you in ways that make him feel good, too. Being together can be fun if you don't work too hard at it. Your growing faith in yourself as a capable parent is important for your baby's development as well as your own, now and later.

# 4. COMMUNICATION: BABBLERS' CHALLENGE

Have you ever noticed how communication varies in families? Some homes are boisterous with lots of talk and laughter. Others are so quiet that one wonders where everyone is. A father we know allows no conversation at mealtime. Whenever anyone in his family starts to say anything at the table, he says, "Be quiet and eat your food." Other families talk over everything at dinner time, and encourage their children from their earliest days onward to openly discuss things that concern them.

Children learn to communicate as their parents do. If yours is a chatty family, the chances are that your children will become so too. For from babyhood on children "pick up" the ways and the pace and tone of communication from their relationships with their parents.

*The mood of your home is set by the tone of your interaction.* Sometimes, when everything is going well, you feel good about yourself and your dear ones. Then your communication may be filled with "purr words" as your loving feelings spill over into the way you reassure one another by tone of voice and fond sentiments. At other times, you feel out of sorts, and then one or the other of you may take to using "slur words" that express your unhappy mood. Such feelings are contagious and run through a family in amazingly short periods of time. Some families become so accustomed to happy positive feelings, or to degrading negative ones, that you can feel the emotional tone of the home as soon as you enter it.

A child growing up in a happy home learns the habit of happiness expressed in it quite as easily as he acquires the language of the family. Your challenge as young parents is to encourage your youngsters to communicate easily and well. Even more it is to provide the emotional climate that facilitates their becoming well-adjusted, outgoing persons. All this begins very early in life—long before the baby learns to speak.

## Wordless Communication

You do not need words to get through to one another. The expression on your face tips off those who know you as to how you feel and what you think about them at the moment. Some of your most powerful emotions are expressed not by words, but by gestures, body posture, and facial expressions. These nonverbal ways of expressing yourself get through to others around you rapidly and affect their responses to you.

*Baby soon masters the art of wordless communication.* By the time he is a week or two old, his eyes search your face and follow your eyes intently. As you cuddle him, he snuggles even closer, pressing his little body against yours. This makes you feel even more loving, and you respond by patting and caressing him. Long before he is able to say "I love you," he has learned to pat you in loving response.

Sometime in the first few months, he learns to pull away from you. You keep him waiting too long for his food when he is hungry, and he reacts by becoming angry with you. When you do finally pick him up, his body stiffens, and his mad cry reproaches you for your apparent neglect. He may turn his face to the wall as you come toward him, letting you know in no uncertain terms that he does not like you very much just then.

Let your baby know that you are sorry you were delayed in coming to tend to his needs, and he "forgives" you by accepting your attention and relaxing with you again. Research shows that the more attentive you are to your baby's needs, the less crying he does. Mothers who are responsive to their baby's signals of distress tend to have happier babies who cry less, than do those whose babies have to fight for what they need.

During your baby's first two years, he learns to respond to you as you have taught him. You love him and let him know it, and he becomes a loving little happy child. You pat and caress him, and his whole body learns to respond. You talk to him, and soon he is replying with coos of his own.

This is the period of his life when your baby begins to signal you with his hands. He points to something he wants—a toy or something to eat. He rubs and fingers a place that hurts—a tummyache or an earache. He pulls you toward him to show you something. He pushes you away when he wants to do something on his own. His newfound confidence in his growing powers make him independent at times. This is a sign that he has enough built-in faith to cope by himself with an ever growing number of situations.

*You are wise to encourage his independence,* as your baby begins to want to do things for himself. You need not feel hurt that he is rejecting your help. You can rejoice with him in his newfound competence. This is a challenging time for many a mother who unconsciously hates to see her baby grow up. Without realizing it, she may discourage his efforts to become independent of her. She hovers over him, tells him he is not big enough yet for whatever it is he is trying to do, and in many other ways tries to keep him a baby as long as she can. You communicate your confidence in him, when you let him take over as soon as he shows he is ready to begin to try.

## How Baby Learns to Use Words

Someone has said that a human being begins to use words as a parrot and may end by creating the language of a poet. Whether he becomes a poet or not is dependent on many influences inside and outside his home. His learning to speak the language of your home is a complex process that goes on for many months of his interaction with you. Actually a baby learns not as a parrot, simply mimicking the words he hears. His use of words evolves partly from the noises he makes, partly from those you respond to, and partly from his repetition of those sounds he hears you use.

A tiny baby expresses his discomfort in cries that are mostly vowels. Sometime later he adds such consonants as "w" (Waaa) to his distress signals. When he is relaxed and happy, his vowels (a, o, u) are often mumbled and mouthed. Early in his repertoire of sounds are the "Mmmmm" noises associated with his pleasure in sucking. When this "m" sound is combined with one of the vowels he knows, it comes out "Mama." This may create a sensation in the family, as the mother hastens to report that the baby has spoken his first word. She smiles and tells him what a big boy he is. This encourages him to use the same combination again and again, until the word "Mama" is established as the beginning of his vocabulary.

"P" and "D" are early consonants a baby uses. These combined with the "Aaaa" sounds he has been using since soon after his birth, emerge as "Papa" or "Dada," which are heralded as his recognition of his father. The proud daddy brags about what a bright baby he has and gives the baby positive reinforcement for continuing to use the word "Papa" or "Dada."

There are many other nonsense sounds and "words" that are not recognized and reinforced by the baby's parents. In time these are discarded in favor of the ones that his parents respond to positively. In another language, it might be these that would be heard and rewarded by praise. Thus it is that the baby in communication with his parents, from the first few months on, learns the beginning of speech.

*"Babbling is the production of meaningless vocal sounds* characteristic of infants from about the sixth week," according to my dictionary. These repetitive sounds appear to be uttered for their own sake when the baby is relaxed and content. He lies in his crib and amuses himself by playing with the sounds he can make. This random vocalizing increases rapidly through the first year. He uses them during his feedings, and "talks back" while his needs are being met. He begins to imitate the sounds he hears around him—over the radio, the television set, and particularly from the special people in his life, you his parents.

Sometime early in his second year, your baby seems to be talking in full paragraphs. He babbles on and on in the same rhythms you use, until he sounds as though he is truly talking. You find yourself straining to hear what he is saying. You feel you could understand if only you try. What he is doing is practicing the "music" of speech long before he has all the words to go with it.

When your baby begins to get around the house, and especially to walk, his talking accelerates. He learns many new words. He uses a single word to convey a whole complicated idea. Then the word "go" sends him into ecstacies of readying himself for a trip with you. We once asked our four-year-old grandson to *Go* to the store with us, and were amused to find his two-year-old sister at the door (her hat on backwards) all ready to go along with us.

By the time your baby is two years old, he may be adept at combining words into his first real sentences. He may say, "Baby car" to indicate his eagerness to go with you in the car. He now can wave "bye-bye" to those he is leaving, with intelligent speech and gesture. He says, "All gone" when playing peekaboo, or when his milk is finished, or someone leaves the room, signifying that he not only can use the words but also knows their meaning in a number of differing situations.

Your baby learns to talk, and you are there to watch it all. How he masters the complex art of speech (as no animal can) is something to marvel at, to rejoice in, and to encourage from the first. Your future communication with this individual may well reflect how good a start you both had in getting through to one another in his infancy. My own hunch is that the "generation gap" is not so much a problem of adolescence, as it is in the earliest beginnings of communication in the family.

## Communication Has to Be Two-way

Do you know the joy of feeling that someone really listens to what you are saying? When the other person responds in a way that lets you know he has heard what you are saying and knows what you meant by it, you glow with what it means to be really understood. How different is the experience of travelling in a foreign land and trying hard with little or no success to communicate with its people in their native tongue. Then you find yourself gesturing, pantomiming, and shouting a single word in an effort to make yourself understood. When you fail, you feel left out, cut off, incommunicado. A baby's experience is like that while he is learning to talk. He replies with delight when he has been heard. He reacts with frustration when he appears not to be understood.

*Communication is a mutual process* of interaction between two or more persons. You must be heard and understood in order to get your meaning across to the other. You in turn must listen and respond appropriately to what he is saying (by word or action) in order to give him the feeling that you hear and understand him. This two-way interaction is especially important during the period when the baby is trying hard to communicate in the language spoken in his home, language that still is foreign to him.

Your infant may get angry when he tries in vain to make you understand something that he is not yet able to communicate clearly. A visiting child in our home threw a temper tantrum when we could not understand what he wanted when he asked for a "Wheel." We brought all manner of wheeled objects: his walker, his pull-toys, even the little sweeper, which only threw him into wilder frustration. Finally, another youngster interpreted what we had heard as "Wheel," as "Wheat" and brought him a bowl of wheat cereal which he accepted with both tears and smiles. The tears, no doubt because it had been so hard to make himself understood; and the smiles that at last he had what he had wanted all along.

Other children often understand what a baby is trying to say better than do adults. Young children can sometimes interpret one another to grown-ups in ways that are mutually helpful. Twins oftentimes are said to develop their own personal language by which they "talk" to one another in ways that few outsiders can understand. One of the joys of childhood and of adolescence is that of using language that they understand but which adults find confusing. "Pig Latin" is an example of school children's attempts to talk in ways that only they understand. The "slanguage" that appears with each new crop of teenagers is another example of how adolescents deliberately try to exclude others by developing a vocabulary that is meaningless to outsiders.

*Concepts are a tremendous breakthrough* in learning to communicate. You can be in on the excitement of his discovery that lots of objects quite unrelated can be *round*. His first experience with "round" may have been with his ball. Then one day he learns that his plate also is round. Finally, he gets the idea of roundness, and trots around the room pointing gleefully to all sorts of things that share the common characteristic of being round. Once he has the feeling of concepts, his learning and his language grow by leaps and bounds. He adds to his collection of concepts: redness, flatness, fullness, heaviness, bigness, tallness—all communicating meanings that he and others understand. His ability to talk now leaps ahead at a fast pace, as he finds that he can relate to you and make a difference in his world and its relationships.

### You Communicate How You Feel About Your Baby

Never assume that because your baby cannot yet talk clearly that he cannot understand what is being said about him. He can understand many words that he cannot speak as yet. Even earlier, he catches the mood of what is being said and reacts to it.

A baby born into a family where he knows he is loved and wanted responds by enthusiastically becoming a real part of the family as soon as he can. You communicate your feeling of joy in him as a wonderful gift of God, and your child responds with all the exuberance of which he is capable. He is busy building relationships with you from his very first day. He adds rapidly to his repertoire of communication as he starts to speak. He gaily goes out to others with a sense that they too will love and respond to him. He seeks new adventures in every possible way, as he grows rapidly in his comprehension of himself, his world, and his people. His intelligence develops rapidly as he learns to communicate. He becomes a real person, to be considered, and reckoned with, and he loves it!

*Each child communicates in his own special way.* Some babies relate to their family more smoothly than do others. It is hard to acknowledge that you respond to any one child differently than you do to another. But you are wise to recognize that your reactions vary whether you admit them or not. Your baby responds to the way you communicate with him, without your using a single word.

If yours is an openly affectionate family, you probably will have a loving, responsive baby. But occasionally there is a hard-to-love child who struggles against you when you attempt to hold him close. He resists your efforts to cuddle him and stiffens his little body when you pick him up. You must develop a great deal of patience in rearing such a child, because his way of relating is not yours, and he appears to reject you and what you try to do for him. In time, you may want to get professional counseling on how to handle the many difficult situations that arise between you and the child "who does not seem to fit" into your family; for he makes it difficult for you, for himself, and for the whole family. His ability to communicate freely has an important effect on the rest of his development, both now and in the future.

## Why Communication Is So Important

Being in touch with other persons is important at any age. Individuals who lose contact with their fellows are lonely, unhappy persons, more often than not.

Mentally ill and maladjusted children and adults are often those who have little or no ability to communicate freely even with those who are closest to them in a physical sense. You see them lost in their own reveries, with very little interaction with their fellows in many a psychiatric ward.

Communication is especially important during the first of life when basic patterns of social interaction are being established. The baby who is lovingly cared for, responds actively to his caretakers, and becomes an outgoing person. The baby who is neglected and left to his own devices tends to withdraw and to become a solitary little individual. Babies who have access to other children develop better socially than do those who do not.

Two-way contact with other persons is necessary for a baby to become truly human. He is born with all the potentials of humanness. But these are developed through his relationships with other human beings. He depends upon his parents not only for physical care, but also for the intimate interaction that encourages his personality development. He looks to them for models of how to respond to a wide variety of situations. When they show fear, he is afraid. When his mother is happy, he tends to be also. When the rest of the family is active, he usually wants to be where the action is, right with them.

Communication is learned in the reciprocal action of two or more persons. When satisfying ways of getting through to one another are established early in a child's life, they tend to continue on through the years. This ability to communicate is a precious heritage. It is one of the greatest gifts you can give your child.

### Helping Your Baby Learn to Communicate

Your baby smiles at everyone until he is about six months of age. Then he begins to turn away from strangers; and to respond enthusiastically only with those he knows. Before he is one year old, he excitedly "talks to" familiar persons. He smiles at members of his family. He clings to his mother and buries his head in her lap. He lifts his hands to his parents to be picked up. Mothers and fathers who are especially responsive to their baby's needs tend to help their little one establish the important close bond upon which further development is based.

*Learning to talk is a complex skill* that is learned gradually from your baby's first year on. You help him to learn to talk by talking to him long before he can use words himself. You encourage his speech as you respond to the sounds he makes, as you name things he expresses interest in, as you read to him, and as you supply him with a wide variety of stimulating objects. The wider his experience, the more he is motivated to talk. It will take time for him to learn the words for things and to express meaningfully the words he knows. Forming true sentences comes a bit later as he combines words in ways that make sense to him and to you. You give him a sense of the power of speech as you give him what he asks for and express with him delight in his growing ability to make himself understood.

*A child's vocabulary grows as he grows.* Books, records, trips, and anything else that give a little child new experiences, enlarge his ability to communicate with you and others. When you accept the feelings that accompany his verbal and nonverbal communication, you even further enhance his ability to get through to others fully and freely.

You parents, more than any other teacher your child will ever have, teach him the fundamentals of human interaction, long before he goes to school. He picks up the conversational tone and richness and patterns of your family speech. He learns either to clam up or to express himself when he feels intense emotion, depending on your acceptance of him as he is. He learns socially acceptable ways of speaking and expressing his feelings from you. When you fly off the handle, he probably will too. As you vent your more violent emotions constructively, while admitting their presence, you are giving him a valuable model on how to handle his. Your ways of expressing joy tend to become his. Your reverence for life he absorbs quite as fully.

Communication is not just polite conversation. It is the stuff of human interaction and development. It is the basis for true prayer. The longing to be in touch with the heavenly Father begins as a child finds satisfying his communication with his earthly parents. How hard it is for a child to feel close to the Lord, when he has little intimate contact with his own father. How difficult it can be to lift his voice in gladness when his mother does not seem to care. Your joy in your child tells him of his Father's love, years before he can read the story in the Bible. Your supreme challenge as parents is to give your child the sense of what it means to be a loved and loving child of God.

# 5. CURIOSITY CHASING WITH THE TODDLER

The toddler is on the go at last. As soon as he can get about on his own two feet, he takes off with enthusiasm. He has a whole new world to explore. His confidence in setting forth to look into what is beyond his earlier horizons matches that of Columbus or modern spacewalkers. He has ten hungry fingers eager to get into things. His mouth is still a major port of entry—for anything and everything. His feet carry him into all available nooks and crannies without selectivity. Toddlers have insatiable thirst for knowledge and experience!

## Curiosity—Need to Know

Curiosity is the intense desire to know. It wells up within a child with a tremendous surge of interest. It is one of the reasons why children are so fascinated with so many elements in their surroundings of which adults are not even aware. "Curiosity killed the cat" is the old wives' tale that warns of the dangers in unbridled inquiry. The other side of the coin of curiosity is much brighter—it is the basis of all future learning.

*Inquisitiveness is the foundation of learning.* It is the motivation that sends the scientist into his laboratory. It is the creative thrust that keeps the inventor at his bench. It is the compulsion to know that accounts for mankind's progress. It is the first building block in the educational process for the individual.

Your baby's attitude toward new experiences is being shaped during these days of exploration. If you encourage his looking into things, you provide a sound foundation for his further learning. As you provide a wide variety of things for him to explore, his interest increases and his knowledge of his world and of himself expands rapidly. Curtail his curiosity and you cause him to withdraw and hold back from the new and the strange. Allow him the chance to explore, and you encourage his God-given desire to learn and to grow.

*Your toddler's urge to experiment* is almost compulsive. He tries all kinds of combinations with the materials at hand. He bangs and pounds and handles and tastes and smears anything that yields to his touch. He grabs and pulls toward himself all manner of things both benign and dangerous. He attempts new ways of handling old familiar things. He pushes his crib around the room. He pulls things off the shelves. He practices combinations of objects by putting them inside, around, along side of, above, and beneath one another. Even his meals become further materials to manipulate.

*Eating gives way to messing* for many a toddler. He finds that foods are something to handle, to pound, to smear, and to throw in ways that have exciting dimensions to him now—now, because of this need to learn what he can do and now because his food requirements are not so great as they were early in his life.

Many a mother is distressed to find that her baby's appetite declines as he nears the end of his first year. Favorite foods are refused or dabbled with. He is not so interested in his milk. Mealtime in general may become a battle between baby and his mother. You may be comforted to know that your baby's food requirements are not so great now as they were the first few months of his life. He continues to grow, of course, but at a slower rate than he did earlier. In fact, he never again will grow as fast as he did at first. So, he does not need as much to eat as he may have eaten with gusto just a few weeks before.

Your toddler's interest in seeing what he can do with things, is expressed in messing with the food he does not want. If you do not like this kind of behavior, you can make a scene, slap his hands, and push food into his resisting mouth. Or, you can recognize what his messing is saying—that he has had enough to eat at the moment. So, you quietly remove the food before him, take him out of his chair, and let him go play, as he so obviously is trying to do.

Once you get the message of your toddler's messing, you give him smaller portions of food. You let him have his own spoon to use. You provide other things for him to smear and manipulate. You keep mealtime calm by not insisting that he eat what he does not want. Pushing food into his mouth that he refuses to swallow only distresses you and encourages him to resist you further. You can be reassured that your toddler will get enough to eat, if you do not make a scene about it. Establishing a pleasant atmosphere in connection with eating is important for you both. It helps at the moment, and it sets the scene for happy mealtimes ahead.

## Getting Around the First Two Years

Your baby was born a tiny helpless infant, unable to hold his head up. Before he is two years old, he is running around the house like the toddler he or she now is. What happens in between the complete helplessness of the newborn and the enthusiastic run-about is an intriguing story that you can watch unfold.

*Learning to walk does not have to be taught a child.* He learns to get about on his own in a process that follows a predictable sequence. First a newborn struggles to get his head up. His chest and back are next in the sequence of movement from horizontal to vertical. A little later your baby begins to make stepping motions when you hold him up. He kicks his legs, and strengthens the muscles that one day will support his full weight. By now he can sit propped up in an infant seat or against a pillow. Sometime near the middle of his first year, your baby can sit in a high chair, and alone when you place him on the floor. From the sitting position, your infant finds that he can pull himself up beside a chair or table or bed—his first effort to stand erect all by himself.

*Creeping and crawling are preliminary to learning to walk.* Before the end of his first year, your baby begins to creep, or crawl, or hitch himself along the floor. These efforts are important in his learning to walk. Crawling is necessary in establishing the dominance of either right or left side of his body. You may wish that your baby would not get so dirty creeping about the floor, but it is essential to his further development. So, put him or her in washable simple rompers and let the baby cruise about in his own pace and way.

Babies differ in the age at which they start to creep and to get about. They vary too in the ingenious ways they try at first to navigate. Some hitch along on their buttocks. Occasionally a baby tries a crab-like movement. Swimming motions are tried by most babies as they rock on their tummies. In time your baby learns what works best for him and makes progress with it. Generally, a baby creeps in his first year, walks in his second, and runs about before the end of his second year. You don't need to worry if your baby does not duplicate the timetable in somebody's book. He will walk when he is ready.

*Toddlers are unsteady on their feet.* Your child is uncertain when he first starts to walk. He spreads his feet in order to balance himself. His legs are still short, and his head and body are big in proportion, so his center of gravity is high. This makes him top-heavy and easily upset. Partly because he has to learn to balance himself and is not yet expert at walking, your baby takes his share of tumbles while he is learning to walk. Left to his own devices, a toddler falls, picks himself up, and starts off again without interruption.

You can encourage this healthy try-and-try-again attitude by *not* running to pick up your toddler every time he takes a tumble. When he slumps to the floor, you can calmly smile at him, reassuring him that he is all right, and go about your activities while he gets on with his walking. You may have to encourage visiting relatives and friends in the same casual attitude lest they run to pick the toddler up every time he loses his balance.

*Climbing up and out is a new adventure* for the toddler. He finds that he can climb out of his chair, his crib, and other places where you have placed him. He learns to climb up on drawers, chairs, tables, and cupboards in a whole new dimension around the house. This is an exciting game for him. And, it adds new levels of responsibility for his caretakers. For now all sorts of things are within the toddler's reach.

Falling from heights can hurt. You now may want to be near to reassure your toddler that he is all right even though he did hurt himself in his fall. He needs your comfort now especially. If he has had a nasty fall that worries you, do not hesitate to call for help—the paramedics in your neighborhood, your doctor, or nearby clinic or hospital. Otherwise cleaning a small cut or open wound, applying a mild antiseptic and a plastic strip with comforting kiss-to-make-it-well is the best treatment.

### Experience Leads to Further Exploration

Growing children need expanding experiences. The more stimulating environment a youngster has, the more curious and interested he becomes. Studies show that children with few things to manipulate become withdrawn and uninterested in the world around them. Those with a rich and varied collection of objects to handle develop confidence in using them, and even more curiosity and interest in exploring.

*Toddler toys can be many and varied.* This is the time when push-pull toys come into their own. A toddler can sense the power of pulling his toy after him, at the same time that he has something to hang onto. This gives him both confidence and the fun of accomplishment. Boxes or cartons that he can drag around into various formations, climb onto, crawl off of, and get into, all are of interest to the toddler.

*Water play has a special attraction* to youngsters at this stage of development. This can center in the bathtub or backyard plastic shallow pool. Cups to pour out of, squeeze plastic bottles to squirt water from, floating rubber and plastic toys to push around, and his own washcloth to bathe with are appropriate. Precautions to follow are several. Remain in sight and sound of the child in the tub at all times. Make sure that there is no electric appliance near enough for the toddler to drag it into the tub with him. Avoid anything that can break, has sharp edges, or can be bitten off and swallowed. At this stage your toddler is exploring with all senses and needs to be protected from things that might harm him.

*Toys that make a variety of sounds* can be considered now. A toddler may enjoy his own little record player onto which he can put his own unbreakable children's records. Favorite records on the big record player may be called for again and again. Toys to bang, drums to beat, bells to ring, are limited to what the adults' ears can stand, but they bring pleasure to almost any youngster of this age.

*Messing and smearing materials* can be introduced now. Sand to play in with a few unbreakable containers that have no sharp edges give an imaginative child a wide variety of experiences. Play-dough that can be purchased or made at home is fun. He or she may be ready for his own cookies to pat down when you are baking. It may be a bit early for finger-paint from your point of view, but your child will love splashing it about and getting both hands into it, if you allow such messing. Putting the toddler into a discarded old shirt and covering the floor with newspapers are helpful in protecting him and the surroundings.

*Mother's presence encourages exploration,* according to recent research studies. When his mother is close by, a toddler moves about and manipulates more freely than he does when she is not watching. Many toddlers find separation from their mothers frightening. They cry for her, reach out toward where they last saw her, and try to follow her when they can.

Some toddlers are more courageous than others, as you may have observed. These brave ones venture forth readily whether mother is watching or not. They "get into everything" whether or not it has been offered them. They seem to be utterly fearless, except when they are tired, or not feeling well, when they cling and seek to be comforted.

First-born children are apt to be somewhat more fearful than other children in the family. Their younger brothers and sisters have them to model after and apparently learn a great deal by watching their older siblings. At any rate, they tend to be more friendly and more venturesome than the only or the oldest child in the family. Boys have been found to be somewhat more fearless than girls, but this may or may not be true in any one family.

## Safeguarding Your Things from Toddler Damage

There is a familiar phrase in child development literature—child-proofing. This refers both to protecting your possessions from damage during your toddler's exploration of the home and safeguarding him from harm he may find in and about the household.

*Child-proofing your home* begins with your willingness to put your toddler ahead of your things in your value system. While he or she is going through the "getting into everything" stage, you put away your most precious possessions. You pack away the breakables that might get broken. You remove the ashtrays and knickknacks. You take out of harm's way anything that your toddler might drop, soil irrevocably, wet harmfully, or otherwise damage.

Floors may be covered with indestructible surfaces, or with washable carpeting in colors that do not show dirt. Walls can be covered with washable plastics, papers, or paints. Slipcovered or Scotch-guarded furniture may be washed when it gets soiled. Drawers and cupboards that must be out of bounds for the toddler may be locked, at least temporarily. There are some ingenious latches that adults can undo that prove inaccessible to all but the most persistent toddler.

Aprons (for you), bibs and old shirts (for the toddler), and washable clothing for members of both generations keep mealtime and messing spills from becoming discouraging for you. Having your laundry area close by the kitchen or bathroom, allows you to throw into the washer, or handy container of detergent, soiled garments as they are removed. This gets them out ot the way and makes their washing easier.

### Protecting Your Toddler from Hazards

You can play a game of trying to see things from your toddler's point of view. Get to some potential hazard before he does and remove it and you win. He gets there first and you have to remove him, and neither of you win.

*The kitchen is full of danger for toddlers.* So, hang all knives high on a wall. Keep pan handles turned in rather than out. Teach your child that burner handles are a strict no-no that he may *not* touch. Keep matches on high shelves. Put a child-proof latch on the cupboard under the sink; or store bleaches, polishes, insecticides, cleaning compounds, ammonia, lye, and other products usually kept under the sink, up where the toddler cannot reach them. Fence off the little child's play area (nearby where you can see each other) from the main traffic lines in the kitchen, or provide high-chair play during mean preparation.

*Your bathroom needs careful attention* in child-proofing. Clear the under washbowl area of all products that are potentially harmful to the toddler. Provide low steps up to the washbowl and low hooks for his towel, washcloth, and cup, so that he can care for his own needs. As soon as he indicates that he is ready, place a potty chair near the toilet for him. Put his water toys in a net bag near the bathtub, so that he can get them himself and so that they can be kept from getting under foot.

*Gates at top and bottoms of stairs* are necessary until your child learns to climb up and down reliably. Bars, tight screens or other safeguards are needed on all windows from which he might fall. Cap electric outlets that he could possibly reach, and fence off electric cords with heavy furniture as much as you can. Keep doorways gated or doors closed so that your toddler will not be tempted to go exploring outside without being accompanied.

*Street traffic has to be a strict no-no* for any toddler. Teach him early to hold your hand and look both ways for cars as you approach the curb. Let him know clearly that he is *not* to go into the street alone for anything. This can be done without frightening him. You do not want an anxious child shivering with fear on the curb; just a careful one who has learned one of the basic rules of safety.

*Emergency precautions* are helpful in even the most careful family. Regardless of how safety-conscious you are, there are bound to be accidents with little children around. Therefore, keep the telephone numbers of your nearest paramedics, your doctor, the local hospital, fire, and police by your telephone. If possible, take a course in home nursing and put your manual where it can be found as needed. If you are near a body of water a Red Cross course in water safety and life saving lessons might be wise. Avoid panic in any of the little accidents that occur. Try to remain calm so that your child will not develop unhealthy fears and anxieties.

## Avoiding Unnecessary Fears

Your little child soon learns to be afraid of the things you fear. If you hide your head under a pillow when a thunderstorm comes, your toddler quite likely will too. As you weather the little storms that brew in your home with poise, the chances are that your children will also.

*Being afraid of the dark* is an almost universal experience of early childhood. You can't talk a child out of it. Turning on the light and showing him that there are no lions by his bed does not convince him. While he, or she, is going through this phase, a night-light will greatly help. It need not be bright, just enough to reassure the child as long as he needs it. Sitting with your child at bedtime and talking with him about the pleasant things he has done that day help put him in a happy frame of mind for sleep. This practice is a good one throughout a child's first ten or more years, as a time for the day's appraisal, and preparation for the night ahead. This is the natural time for prayers, aloud with mother or father, in the child's own language as well as those he has been taught.

*Fear of some specific object or animal* may crop up in spite of all your efforts to avoid frightening your child. Such a fear may be overcome in time. You can gradually recondition your child to be less afraid of dogs, or cats, or birds, or whatever by giving him something pleasant to do at the time that the feared animal appears. Making the child go to the creature that he fears is needlessly cruel and may only intensify his anxiety. Insisting that a trembling toddler pat the big dog that he is afraid of, is not nearly so helpful as reassuring the toddler that the dog looks big to you too, but that you can both eat your cookies and watch the dog from a safe distance.

### Essential No-Nos

Toddlers have to have definite limits. For their own safety, they must be clearly taught what they may not do. These forbidden activities include such things as the following.

*Toddlers should be kept out of the garage and driveway.* There they face the hazard of being struck by a moving automotile as they play beneath or behind a car. Father's workshop should be out-of-bounds for the toddler. Too much of his equipment is hazardous for a young child. Run-about children should not be allowed on or near the kitchen range where they might be burned by hot utensils, flames or burners. They have to be kept out of front-loading washers and dryers into which they might crawl without notice. Refrigerators and freezers in use must be made child-proof, for their protection. Discarded ice boxes and similar air-tight containers should be removed from the premises entirely. You will find other dangerous situations in your household that you forbid to your toddler.

*How you teach a toddler to stay away* from hazards is important. The first time you see your toddler approach an area that is forbidden, calmly take him by the hand and tell him "No-no." It is wise to add a simple one-word reason why this has to be a restricted area for him. You can say as he approaches the stove, "No-no—hot." When he again comes near, be sure to forbid him by repeating your warning. Be consistent in training your toddler, and he will learn quickly that you really mean what you are saying.

*Your toddler may tease you* by playfully seeming to do the thing you have forbidden. Long before one of our little boys could talk, we warned him not to touch the front-loading dishwasher. The next several times he entered the kitchen, he headed straight for the dishwasher, put out his hand as if to touch it, turned and laughed at us, as he waved his hand back and forth in front of the door. We laughed at his joke with him, and repeated no-no in a happy tone, congratulating him on having learned so fast. He enjoyed this little game in which he took the initiative in limiting his own conduct, with our approval.

A toddler may be found doing something that is forbidden at the same time that he is saying no-no aloud. Repeating the no-no he has heard is his first step in learning what he may not touch. When you find your toddler telling himself no-no while doing the forbidden, repeat the no-no with him, lead him away and give him some distraction.

*Spanking rarely helps at this age.* You may have to lead him away from the driveway or the street, in no uncertain way. But hitting him only complicates the problem, and confuses the issue for him. There will come a time when a well-placed physical reminder may seem to you like the only thing to impress upon your little one some point you want to emphasize. This is effective *after* he has begun to develop a sense of right and wrong. For now, being limited in his exploration is frustrating enough for the toddler.

*Limit your no-nos to a few absolute essentials.* If everything he touches is a no-no, your toddler will react in one of two ways, neither of which is helpful. Either he will ignore your commands and continue blithely with the forbidden behavior as if he had not heard you. Or, he will respond with such intense frustration that you have an angry child on your hands.

Remember that the toddler is learning from his exploration of his world. This is an urgent need for him right now. When you severely curtail him, he gets mad, and lashes out with unbridled anger. Then you have the original problem further complicated by his tantrum.

### Temper Tantrums

In a temper tantrum, a toddler reacts to frustrating interference with kicking, screaming, crying, hitting, and banging anything within reach, even his own body on the floor. He is so upset by being restrained that he loses control completely. Now he is so irrational that appeals to reason are useless. Threatening him, "Be quiet, or you'll have something real to cry about," is usually ineffective.

You best deal with a temper display by calmly removing the youngster from the scene. Dr. Goodenough studied 1,878 temper outbursts of little children and came to the conclusion that their control is best achieved by adult serenity and consistency. When you keep your self-control, your child is helped to regain his. When your discipline is assured and consistent, he learns what he may and may not do, in time.

*Ignoring the toddler's tantrum* works in a situation where it is safe for him to play it out. Giving him too much attention for his temper display only rewards him further. He learns that he can upset you by getting mad, and this reinforces his use of tantrums in trying to control you. Hitting him to "snap him out of it" may simply teach him that hitting is all right. When you ignore his unpleasantness, and pay as little attention to it as possible, he learns that it does not work. He gets over it sooner the less you make of it.

### Coping with Clutter

Your own patience may wear thin with your toddler's clutter. Toddlers are not neat, tidy little people. They love to pull things apart, but they know nothing about putting them to rights again. Anything they play with is left where they dropped it. This makes sense from their point of view. But it is difficult for others in the family.

*Your pick-up policy reflects your philosophy* of parenthood. If you chase after your toddler, cleaning up behind him, fussing about the mess he is making, you may have a neat house, but a nervous, unhappy youngster. Restrain him from the exploration that comes naturally for him, and you limit his learning and hinder his development.

The best thing you can give your toddler is the freedom to be himself. If you can share your home with this inquisitive new little member, with a minimum of restraint, you are to be congratulated. For, letting a toddler explore and manipulate, roam and rummage, touch and taste, pull and push, climb and clutter allows him to express his eagerness to be at home in your home at this age.

There will be many years ahead in your family when you can have a well-kept house. There is only *now* for your toddler in which to absorb what he must know about himself and his environment. So, insofar as you can, put your child first, and let your housekeeping slacken off for awhile.

# 6. WORKING AT PLAY WITH TWO- THROUGH FOUR-YEAR-OLDS

The summer Linda was two she was given a little aluminum tea set, consisting of cups, saucers, sugar, creamer, teapot, and one small plate. For some time after she got the tea set, she played with it in the backyard wading pool. She poured from cup to cup. She filled the teapot and poured from that. She then began to pour from teapot to cup, running it over more often than not. Finally she was able to gauge her pouring so that she could pour a cupful of water without spilling any. Then a whole new game began.

About this time, her grandparents arrived for a visit. They were scarcely seated before Linda appeared with "tea." Her grandmother accepted the tiny cup of "tea" with a smiled, "Thank you, Linda." Linda burst into a bright smile, and ran to get tea for her grandfather. He too thanked her, and she wiggled with pleasure, stood facing him for a long moment as though to make sure that he would bring the cup to his lips. He promptly did, at which Linda ran from the room and returned with cup after cup for her parents and older brother.

This play went on for weeks. As soon as someone was seated, Linda would bring "tea." Her cousin about her age came and he joined in the game when Linda asked him to pass the "cake." He solemnly followed each cup of proffered "tea" with the outstretched little plate. A visiting aunt in the spirit of the play asked one afternoon if she could have sugar for her tea. Then a new dimension appeared with sugar and creamer added to the children's hospitality.

One day Linda's brother failed to thank her for his cup, and she complained that he had forgotten to say thank you. He replied that he was tired of her old tea parties and didn't want anymore. The saddened Linda retreated to her chair for several minutes. After this, she approached each new guest not with the cup, but with a smiled, "Like, tea?" When the answer was yes, she would dash from the room and return almost at once with cup and saucer, Mark in tow with the cake plate, and then both children one with sugar and the other cream.

Just playing, you say? Don't you believe it. Linda and Mark worked at their tea party game until they had it perfected. They were so busy learning so many things that summer that they dropped into bed exhausted each evening. What a lot two-to-four-year-olds have to learn. Child development specialists have listed a dozen or more tasks that children this age must master.

*Development tasks are the growth responsibilities,* the jobs to to be accomplished, at each stage of children's development. When the children succeed, they are pleased with themselves. When they fail, they are unhappy, and try again. Parents who work at their children's play with them, help them accomplish their many developmental tasks that must be done at each stage of their growth in order for them to proceed to the next stage of their development successfully. Some of the developmental tasks for two-to-four-year-olds are:

( 1 ) Settling into healthful daily routines of rest and activity;
( 2 ) Mastering good eating habits;
( 3 ) Learning the basics of toilet training;
( 4 ) Developing appropriate physical and motor skills;
( 5 ) Becoming a participating member of the family;
( 6 ) Beginning to conform to others' expectations;
( 7 ) Expressing healthy emotions in a variety of situations;
( 8 ) Learning to communicate with increasing numbers of others;
( 9 ) Coping with dangerous situations;
(10) Developing initiative and a sense of self;
(11) Becoming comfortable as a boy or a girl; and
(12) Laying foundations for understanding the meanings of life.

You may enjoy seeing how many of these developmental tasks Linda was working on with her tea party play. There are at least eight, and possibly nine, of these jobs to be accomplished at her age that she was at work on in her tea party game. She was fortunate in having a family that patiently went along with her play which involved them. Had she been ordered "outdoors to play" at a critical point in her learning, her "work" might have been interrupted.

## Joining in the Spirit of Play

There are at least three types of little children's play in which their parents may be actively involved. These are: (1) Dramatic, acting-out play in which youngsters put into action skills they are learning, and they may be practicing future roles. This was central in Linda's tea party play. (2) Music and dance which centers in developing a sense of rhythm and enjoyment. (3) Creative play in which a child produces something uniquely his own.

*Dramatic play is seen in many variations* among two-to-four-year-olds. They play house, tea party, laundering, bathing, baby-feeding, parent-child discipline (as when a child scolds her doll or pet). They play postman, fireman, policeman, and rescue squads. They play school, church, and hospital. Currently their play often includes moon walks and space exploration, complete with countdowns and landings. One mother reports that her son could count down from ten to one before he learned to count from one to ten.

Each of these variations in dramatic play is apt to follow some new idea that a child has from an experience in the family, a television program, or a trip he has taken. His father reprimands him, and he uses the same tone of voice in scolding his dog. Her mother answers the phone, and the little girl talks over her toy (or pretend) phone with the same inflections. The children see television programs of space explorations, and their play soon reflects that new experience. A shopping trip stimulates playing store. A physical checkup brings forth playing doctor, hospital, and giving shots. A fire in the neighborhood is played out over and over again with sirens, fire engines, climbing men, and rescuing valuables.

Perceptive parents observe these dramatic productions of their children with responsive pleasure. When they are invited to participate, they can enjoy going along with the game, as Linda's parents and grandparents did. When they become aware of the little child's need for new experiences to stimulate his imaginative play, they see the reason for taking him along on errands and trips with them. Less responsive parents unwittingly discourage a little child's learning through play by being in too much of a hurry to bother with a tag-along youngster.

*Imaginary playmates serve many a child's needs.* Studies show that between one fourth and one third of little children have an imaginary playmate, at least for awhile. Bright children are more likely to talk about their imaginary playmates. Girls more than boys tend to fantasy their own playmates. In adolescence more creative teenagers report having had imaginary playmates when they were young. College students who had had imaginary playmates as children are found to be friendlier, more cooperative, have higher grades and stronger feelings than do those who have had no childhood companions of their own fabrication.

Parents are wise not to discredit their child's imaginary companion. They may accept the new member of the family, by not sitting in the chair in which the imaginary playmate is, or by doing what they can within reason to respect their youngster's pretend-companion. One mother we knew drove to the bus to pick up her child's "Teresa" who came for a visit. The little girl welcomed her gaily, and chatted with her all the way home in the car. Teresa stayed for ten days, and then quietly left without a trace. Other imaginary playmates may stay for longer or shorter periods of time. They usually are there because the child needs them: for company, as a model, as a scapegoat, or as someone to talk to when conversation is the agenda of the time for the youngster.

*Little children enjoy music.* A two-year-old may sing to himself as he plays. He or she may spontaneously go into a little dance when he is happy, or drone a sobbing little song when he is sad. He often sings himself to sleep, and many a child of this age wakens with his own "Goodmorning Song," with or without words.

*Children like to make their own creative productions.* These can be of any shape or form. They are of many materials—whatever is at hand: cookie dough when mother is cutting out cookies, blocks to build with, clay to model with, paints to smear or daub or dribble or brush on, pencil and paper on which to scribble.

*Drawing and writing are complex learnings* that continue for a long while. A little child starts by scribbling in big swirls over the entire surface he can reach. Somewhere between the time he is two and four he begins to try designs of circles, crude squares, and rectangles. Before he goes to kindergarten he usually is drawing things with combinations of the circles and squares he has learned.

Parents encourage a child's writing and drawing by providing him with a variety of materials to use (newsprint and crayons, blackboard and chalk, paper and pencil, and so forth). When mother or father sit down to write, their three-year-old may want, indeed really *need* writing materials also, in order to feel that he or she is participating in the activity.

Parents need not ask a child what he is writing or what it is that he has drawn. They help most when they let the youngster alone with his creation, until he is ready to share it. When a little child brings his production to an adult, the grown-up should not try to correct it for the child or suggest a better way of doing it. It is best simply to ask, "Do you want to tell me about it?" and then listen appreciatively if the child wants to talk about what he has done.

### Seeing Toys as Tools for Learning

As soon as you see toys as tools for the child to use in his work, you have an important criterion for making them available. You do not need to create a fully-equipped toy store for your youngster. It is better by far to choose and make available those toys that are suitable for his present interests and stage of development.

*Toys for dramatic play* can start with cast-off grown-up clothing with which a youngster may play at being an adult. These can be kept in a chest, drawer, or box to which the youngster has access when he wants it. Other tools he or she will need in acting-out play are safe, nonbreakable cups, pitchers, pans of varied sizes and shapes, small cars, trucks, planes, boards for runways, blocks for building garages, schools, houses, stores, counters, and other things with which a youngster can act out the many roles and functions he sees around him.

*Climbing equipment* (ladders, slides, domes, jungle gyms) in the yard serve to help develop large muscle skills, and to dramatize being spacemen, firemen, and animals at the zoo. A slide with or without a shallow plastic pool to slide into is of interest to a small child. So is the beach, or sandbox at which he can mold and pour, make roads and tunnels in moist sand with limitless potential for the imaginative child.

*Clay or play-dough* shapes itself to the child's will. You can buy play-dough in airtight containers that keep it well. Or, you can make it at home: 2 cups of flour, 1 cup salt, enough water to make it of stiff dough consistency. Add washable vegetable coloring, and flavoring if you wish. A couple of drops of oil of cloves will add to its keeping qualities. Put it in a plastic bag and it will keep a month or so, by which time it will be too dirty to use further anyway.

You can put your young children into easily washed clothes for their more messy activities with dough, sand, water, paints, and so forth. Cut-down plastic aprons, or an old shirt back to front with sleeves cut short, protect the child's clothes. Layers of newspapers on floor, table, or other working areas safeguard your possessions. Once your child is hard at work on his creation, you will not want to bother him with admonitions to avoid spilling and messing.

*Things that encourage music and rhythmic activities* are already in your home. Your radio, television, piano, organ, record player, harmonica, accordion, or other instruments used by one or more family members draw your two-to-four-year-old to them as soon as he or she hears a familiar tune. As he shows interest, you may want to invest in his own little inexpensive record player on which he may play his unbreakable records of children's songs, marching bands, and the rest. In time, you may be able to tolerate his occasional use of drums or bugle or triangle. But if it annoys you, these can wait until your child gets into nursery school or kindergarten where he can join the rhythm band.

Singing as you work encourages him to follow suit. When someone in the family or neighborhood whistles as he goes about, your youngster will try to also. Spontaneous children's parades down the street stimulate even the littlest ones to join in as soon as they can. Dancing with balloons, in autumn leaves, in the winter's snow, or spring flowers brings joy to children of any age.

*Cuddly toys are comforting.* It may be a beat-up Raggedy Ann doll or a terry cloth lamb, but every youngster at times likes to have something soft to hold close. When he or she is tired, sleepy, or feeling out of sorts there is nothing that takes the place of a familiar Teddy bear or other soft toy that can be cuddled. Linus with his blanket has popularized a universal need of little children—to hold onto something that is their own special comfort when they need it most. Keeping the blanket or comfort-toy clean may be a problem. You can suggest that it is time for the doll to be washed and dried, assuring the child that it will be all ready very soon. It is best not to try to secret it away or discard it without telling the child, and preparing him for its loss, even temporarily. A pet is of greatest use to a child when he is old enough to help care for it. So, unless there already is a family dog or cat, or other animal, it may be wise to postpone the child's first one until he is a little older.

## Dealing with Negativism

Your child of two more or less goes through a stage of vigorous negativism that you can find exasperating. Now that he has learned to get around, and fend for himself somewhat, he lets it be known in no uncertain terms that he prefers to do things for himself. He shouts no to your simplest request. You try to dress him and he backs off with a "Can do—ME!" When you attempt to get his feet into his shoes, he curls his toes, and battles your every move. At another time he conforms quite happily to your ministrations until you find it hard to predict his rebellion and to deal with it constructively.

*Your two-year-old is no longer a baby,* and he knows it. Much of the time he is determined to prove that he is an autonomous person in his own right. He is demanding the right to make his own decisions, to stand on his own feet, and to push you off along with your suggestions and efforts to be helpful.

Some parents find it helpful to go along with their negativistic one by making suggestions just the opposite of what they want done. If they want the two-and-one-half-year-old to eat his food, they may say, with a smile, "Don't touch that food." This is a game a negativistic child can understand, and at times he plays it well. In other situations he is too smart, or too tired, or too frustrated to be taken in by such tactics.

*Temper tantrums in two-year-olds* are wild outbursts of anger that are hard to control. If you give him what he is yelling for, you are simply rewarding his unpleasant behavior. If you let him scream and kick, you feel like an inadequate fool, who can't even control a young child. Your best bet is to calmly ignore the temper tantrum as long as you can as you go about your work. When the scene becomes disruptive to you or others, quietly carry the angry youngster to a place by himself where he can complete his tantrum. You may tell him while you are bodily removing him, that as soon as he feels better, you will be glad to have him come back. This kind of handling often brings a child back into the family circle, all affable compliance (until the next outburst). What you are doing in this kind of handling is accepting your child and his feelings, while letting him know that his behavior is not acceptable. Thus he learns that some things are not good to do, while others are.

## Helping a Child Develop a Conscience

Your child was not born with a conscience. He learns what is right and what is wrong from you and the other special people in his life. From his earliest days he found out that some things he did pleased you. These he tended to repeat when he could. He discovered that other things were no-nos that he must not do. Thus before he or she left infancy there was already a budding sense of right and wrong in the baby.

*Your child's conscience is his built-in set of your no-nos* over the years. Set up too many prohibitions and his conscience becomes too tight for comfort. So, he rebels, or he turns you off and doesn't listen anymore. Or, he becomes guilt ridden and neurotic. Establish too few limits and he responds to your permissiveness with confusion, and perhaps with a feeling that you do not care enough about him to protect him. Neither of these outcomes is desirable. So, parents are hard put to help their child develop a conscience that is firm enough to keep his wilder impulse under socially acceptable control and flexible enough to allow him freedom to be himself.

*Preaching, scolding, and reminding your child* helps very little in his conscience development. It takes him the better part of his first five or six years to learn right from wrong, and he does it best at his own pace. Even after he gets in school, he will be refining the rough edges of his conscience, so don't rush him. If he loves you and knows that you love him, he will want to please you. That is your strongest asset in child-rearing.

## Satisfying Your Child's Word Hunger

Someone has said that a little child is as hungry for words for things as he is for food. This probably is an exaggeration. But it is true that most children between two and four, more or less, are eager to learn to talk, to communicate, to use words they hear, and to practice their rapidly growing vocabularies.

*Knowing the names for things* he sees gives a child a sense of power over them. Because he knows their names they seem to belong to him in a special sense. Now he can use the word for something and others understand to what he is referring. By his use of the right word, he has brought the thing inside himself so that he can produce it in communication without actually having it literally there. He says, "Beach," and others know he is thinking about the seashore and would like to go there again. He hears, "Doggie," and is able to "see" a dog whether it is present or not. He now has grasped that words stand for things and actions and ideas that make up the distinctly human world. It is a giant step in his learning to be a human being that no other creature in the world shares.

*Sesame Street and other television programs* for a little child help him satisfy his word hunger. They introduce letters, words, and actions at a pace that a young child can follow, repeat, and learn in ways that have proven effective. First-grade teachers find that children who have watched *Sesame Street* in their preschool years are as much as a year or more ahead of those who have not seen the program. They have learned to identify numbers and letters, to count, to know that everything has a name, and a great many other things they might not have learned without having had the benefit of the program.

When your little child watches this program, you may find it of interest too. It can help you understand some of your child's conversation and activities after seeing a particular program. When you watch it together, at least some of the time, you have a common experience about which to talk.

*Many television programs are unsuitable for children.* Even those supposedly for youngsters are too often filled with violence to merit your approval. Others are beyond a little child's comprehension or too suggestive to be healthful or helpful. You will be wise to know what your little children are watching and set limits that make sense to you as to which programs they may see, as well as how long they may stay in front of the set.

*Answering children's questions* may be time consuming, but it is all important for a little child hungry to know all about things. Some children's questions are easily answered with a simple statement of fact. Others are so complex that the wisest philosopher or theologian would find them difficult. A little child can ask, "Where was I when you were little?" or "Where is the wind going?" or "What does God look like?" and stump all but the most resourceful parent. When the youngster's questions become even more personal, the answers are apt to be still more difficult. This is why sex education is hard for so many parents.

## Sex Education Has Already Begun

You have already taught your child to feel good about his body, to trust you and life itself. This began during his first weeks of life in the way you cared for your baby. You held him close and met his needs, and he felt secure and loved. The way you fed and diapered and bathed and comforted him taught him the basic attitudes toward himself that are the foundation of sex feelings.

*Names for body parts and functions* are sought even before the child can speak the words himself. He touches his nose, and you say, "Nose"; he touches your mouth, and you say, "Mouth." Soon, he is playing the name game eagerly, by touching and expecting from you the name for parts of the body. A short time later, he is ready to use the words himself, and plays with his parents the game of "What's this?" You speak the appropriate noun, and he proudly repeats it himself. The next step is your asking him, "Where's your ear? your nose? your arm? your leg?" and so on, to his delight and yours. You handle well this phase of your child's education when you use such words as "penis," "vulva," "breast," and "anus," as comfortably as you did "nose," "mouth" and "ear." What your child then is learning is the correct name for the parts of his body. Quite as important, he is finding that all of his God-given body is all right. You are teaching him by your open acceptance of everything about him that you like him as he is—all of him.

*Your child's sex education actually begins with your own feelings about him and his body.* Some modern parents go into a period of retraining so that they can meet their children's needs. They want to answer their child's questions without the hang-ups that they may have, as parents. Parent groups may already meet in your community. Your local library has books for parents on how to answer children's questions simply, honestly, and healthfully. You find these of greatest help early in your child's development. You and your baby can get off to a good start in your learning together. You learn most from your child himself as you see life and growth from his point of view, filled with wonder and mystery and the joy of learning and being.

*Answering little children's questions* cannot wait for schoolteachers or doctors. It has to be done at home, where the situations arise. Your young daughter sees her father or a male visitor of any age standing to urinate, and she asks, in one way or another "Why can't I do that?" and "Why are girls different from boys?" Your answer can be a simple one: Boys have penises because they are growing up to be men, and someday will be fathers. Girls grow up to be women who can have babies, so they do not need to have a penis. You couch this simple reply in your own way, of course. You do not need to go into elaborate detail, now. If your answer satisfies your little child, she or he will be back with other questions as they arise.

*"Where did the baby come from?"* or "Where did I come from?" is one of the first questions children ask as soon as they can talk. Your response does not need to be difficult. You go about whatever you are doing, smile, and say, "You grew in your mother, the way all babies do." This is followed almost at once, or sometime later, by the next question, "How did the the baby get out?" Your answer to this is short and simple: "Through a special place in mother's body, the day you were born." Once you have met these first questions well, the others come more easily. Even the emotionally-laden one for many parents: "How do babies get started in their mommies?" can be answered from the child's point of view (which is not so full of past experience and feeling), with: "All babies have fathers who get their babies started." The details of how the father part gets into the mother can wait until later when your child is ready for it.

*You don't need to tell everything at once.* Sex education goes on for many years. It is best approached step by step as your child is ready. Trying to "give the whole story" in one cozy fireside chat is fiction that is rare indeed in real life. Waiting until the child gets to school or is "old enough to find out for himself" is a poor policy. Your child learns most of his attitudes, facts, feelings, and values about sex from you his parents, as he grows up with you, at home. A good school or church program can fill in many of the details, but the foundation has already been homemade—by *you.*

## Making Toilet Training Comfortable

You make toilet training comfortable for yourselves as parents when you realize that you can't rush it. There is little that you can do effectively before your child is two, more or less. Some children are ready before others are to be toilet trained. Girls are a bit easier to train than boys. Their muscles must be mature enough to function reliably. They *have to want to* give up their diapers, and wetting and soiling themselves, before they are truly ready to be trained.

*Your ease in handling dirty diapers* helps you make toilet training comfortable for yourself and your child. If you can relax and cope with daily diapers, without too much fuss and strain, you have half the battle won. Get your household started early in rinsing out soiled diapers as soon as they are removed from the baby. Put them at once into a mild disinfectant solution in a covered container alongside of your toilet, and you simplify laundering them and have little offensive odor. Establish routines of regular diaper-washing, drying and folding, so that you always have dry, clean diapers at hand and no pileup of soiled ones.

*Give your neighbors and relatives a deaf ear* when they try to convince you that your child should be housebroken, or that some other younger child now has been completely toilet trained. You are not raising some other child. You are responsible for your child, and you are wise to follow his lead for when he is ready to give up his diapers for more grown-up practices.

*Your two-to-three-year-old has to learn what it feels like* to need to go to the toilet before he can use it. He must know how to hold his urine and stools. He has to learn how to let them go when he gets to the potty. These are complicated learnings for a little child. Your youngster indicates he is ready for toilet training when he or she begins to like things neat and where they belong. Before this the child enjoys messing and messes—with his toys, his clothes, and himself.

You and your child make toilet training comfortable when you both work together at it. This means that it is best not done when your child is going through a stage of negativism and self-assertion. Wait until he or she is eager to please and the whole thing will be easier, without too much distress to either of you. Praise for success helps, but punishment for failure does not. Remember that your child is doing the best he can and that this, like other learnings, takes time for him to master.

### Bedtime Routines

Bedtime can be a happy period in your home. You avoid the stalling, the calling for drinks of water, and other delaying tactics when your child is happily ready when you tuck him or her into bed. This requires some build-up of readiness. You are wise to let your two-to-four-year-old have a little quiet play after his supper. Then a leisurely bath with his water toys to play with and maybe a bit of a snack while he is being dried. Then toothbrushing and into bed with a few moments of time with one of his parents all to himself.

*Talk about the nice things that happened that day.* Father or Mother can hear the child's prayers; there can be stories, made up about the child and his family, or others like them. A bit of a favorite book can be read. A soft light can be left on, if the youngster wants it, as many children this age do. Then the tucking in, the good-night kiss and hug, the assurance, "I love you," that everyone likes to hear. With cuddly toy held close the child may turn into his favorite sleeping position, ready for you to leave the room. If this all sounds too easy, be assured we know it is not always this simple. But it can be more often if you follow a few cardinal rules for bedtime routines.

*Be firm and kind in keeping to the usual bedtime hour.* If something unusually attractive comes up just at the child's bedtime (a television program he *must* see, favorite drop-in visitors, etc.) you can yield that night, and go back to the regular bedtime thereafter. When you are going out, leaving a sitter in charge, be sure to prepare your child for your absence. Have the sitter come in time to get acquainted with your youngster—perhaps to supervise the child's bathtime. Be there when you can to tuck the youngster in, hear his prayers, and kiss him good-night.

*Avoid hassles and horseplay at bedtime* when possible. Such activities only stimulate the child so that sleep does not come easily. Bed is a pleasant place to be, not a punishment for being naughty or a place to be put when a child is not wanted under foot. Keep the child's day pleasant and active, and he will welcome sleep—as you do, yourself.

## Handling Jealousy Among Children

Older children in the family may notice that their young sibling is allowed greater leeway than they had when they were his or her age. This is often true. Whereas the oldest child used to be tucked into bed at a regular early hour, bedtime becomes more flexible with later children in the family. So too are other rules and practices that may seem like indulgences denied to the older children. You as parents can admit that this increasing ease in rearing children comes with experience. At the same time you can point out some of the advantages of being the older one(s) in the family. Even this will not eliminate the feelings of jealousy, for sibling rivalry is part of having brothers and sisters.

*Children often are jealous of the new baby in the family.* He gets more than his share of mother's time and attention. He cries and isn't big enough to be of interest to the older child. He is stiff competition for the somewhat older brother or sister. Some regression back to being a baby can be expected as a normal reaction, then. The two-to-four-year-old may lapse into wetting himself as the new baby does. He may want a bottle again, and there is no reason why he should not have it, for awhile. Being displaced as the baby in the family is hard for him. Your child needs your loving understanding while he learns to accept the new baby as a real and permanent member of the family.

*Things to pound and hit* help a little child get rid of his jealousy. It does no good to tell him that he really loves the new baby when he seethes with the sad anger of the dispossessed. You help him deal with his true feelings when you let him know that you understand. You might tell him that you know that sometimes he does not like the baby very much; at other times he does—that's the way it is. You can enlist his help in caring for the new baby, by handing you a fresh diaper, or baby powder, or towel when you are bathing the baby. You may give him a cloth or rubber baby doll to punch when he feels like hitting the real baby. He can use clay to model babies with, and then pull off their heads, if he feels like it. This will not really harm anyone, and helps the youngster constructively express his violent emotions. It may help to laugh with your little child about how messy the baby gets himself sometimes. He'll appreciate that, and will feel more grown-up himself, then.

*You can't talk your child out of his real feelings.* You get along best when you understand and accept them as part of the stuff of life itself. This is what the prodigal son's brother went through, in the biblical story. If you can remember the torment you knew as a child when some other child seemed to be preferred over you, it will give you the perspective you need with your own children.

# 7. GOING OUT TO OTHERS WITH CHILDREN

The day your child slips off your lap, he toddles off to a whole new world of other people. Children have a way of introducing their parents to community life as few others can. You get to know the other children in the neighborhood, their pets and their families by name. In the process you learn a great deal that you never knew before about them, about yourself, and about your child.

## Learning to Play with Others

While your child was a little tyke, he played mostly by himself. He, or she, explored everything within reach. Nothing in your home or immediate environs escaped investigation. He got the feel of all sorts of textures, sizes, weights, and flexibility of the things he could touch. He experimented with what could be done with pots and pans, blocks, blankets, the family dog, and himself. In time, he began to master many aspects of environment. By then he was strong enough to get about by toddling, walking, running, and climbing. He was ready now to move further afield, onto the porch, into the yard and the immediate neighborhood. He enjoyed going with you to shop, to visit friends, to see his grandparents. At the first sign of your getting ready to leave the house, he was there at the door, ready to go too. He was all set for the world of other people that lay beyond your home.

*First experience with other children can be rough.* The little child who has played alone the first year or more of his life has to learn how to relate to others. In his first contacts with other children, he treats them like the varied things he has been so vigorously exploring. He pokes and pushes, grabs and grapples with other youngsters as he has done with his toys. Children about his stage of development relate to him with the same exploratory spirit that sometimes can be rough on him. They push him over in their exuberance. He comes crying to you for comfort. You reassure him and he's back with the other youngsters for the next round.

Your child at this stage can hurt others unintentionally. He grabs what he wants, without regard to the other children's feelings. He runs through their play area, scattering their materials. He topples a tower another child has been building. He is especially hard on some older child's project that is in his way.

*What can you, as a parent, do to help?* You do what you can to protect him from being badly hurt. You guide the older children to work on their project out of the toddler's path. You do not need to make a big issue of your little child's initial ruthlessness in his play with others. He soon will learn from the other children that he cannot run roughshod over them. Your too protective interference but delays this natural learning.

By two years more or less, your child plays happily near other children. You see them side by side at the beach or in the sandbox, pouring, shovelling, making truck tracks, and building simple ditches and mounds. The children seem to enjoy playing next to each other, with very little interaction, yet.

*Playing with other children is a big step* for your child. He (or she) probably begins this stage of play somewhere around his third year. He may start much earlier if he has had experience with other children in your home. He may be a little slower if his contact with others has been limited up to then. At first, you see your child move in and out of a group of children who are playing together. Soon he joins in their play with more or less success at first. In time, he and they are talking over what they are doing. They decide who is going to be the pilot and who the passengers of the airplane they are pretending to fly. They find that they have to take turns in order to keep one another in the game.

This is a complicated process for them that they work on over many weeks or months. They are completely absorbed in these activities. Their voices are raised in excitement. Squabbles break out among the children. The loser reacts by throwing his weight around or by running home crying to his mother. She helps best when she takes his injured feelings casually. She reassures him, without judgment, as to who was right and who wrong. She may send him back to the group with some little treat to ease his reentrance into the play.

*Fighting over toys* declines as your child learns to take turns with the others. Here again, the children are their own best teachers. They learn from one another how much selfish grabbing they can get away with safely. They find out how far it is safe to go in riding roughshod over each other. In such power struggles your child is learning to stand up for his rights. He is finding out that other children fight for what they want, as he does. If the toy the struggle is over is his, his sense of possession gives him the edge, and he'll often win the battle over it. When it is some other child's toy he is trying to grab, he feels the fury of the owner's rights.

As a parent, you help most when you let the youngsters work out their problems by themselves. You keep an eye on the proceedings but don't interfere too much. You may step in when some child is getting the worst of it. Then your best course is not to scold or preach, but to take the toy from the struggling children, and remove it temporarily from the scene. If you can be calm and casual about your intrusion, you help the children know that there are limits to physical attacks that responsible adults enforce.

*Sharing comes in time,* when your child is ready for it. Somewhere around his third year, your youngster becomes fond enough of his playmates to want to share with them. Until then, your insistence that he share only aggravates him and may make him even more selfish. When he does voluntarily share something with another child, you can smile at him. You may mention aloud that it is nice to share. When you tuck him in bed that night, you can tell him how pleased you were to see him share his toy with another child. Or, you relate the happy incident to his father when he comes home, so that your youngster sees that sharing is a good thing to do, in the eyes of the whole family.

### What's Funny About Children's Humor?

Children share a world of rituals and humor that few adults know. School-agers have elaborate rituals that pass from one generation of children to the next. Rope skipping and hopscotch chants that most girls use repeatedly have long since been forgotten by their parents. Schoolboy's language is replete with crude words that are offensive to adults, generally. Swear words and terms for body wastes and functions become funny to groups of children, partly because they are forbidden in polite society.

Your function as parents is to discourage your child's vulgarity, without hurting his budding sense of humor. You may take the approach of saying, "We don't think such things are funny." You may be even more casual by telling your child, "I do not like that word, so please do not use it here." The time-honored approach of washing out the child's mouth with soap or punishing him for using four-letter words is not as effective as ignoring the practice, after an initial casual comment like the above.

*Riddles that send children into gales of laughter,* often sound silly to adults. At a recent children's gathering, a ten-year-old's riddle won the acclaim of his peers, while the parents in the room appeared completely baffled. The question was "What is white on the outside, green on inside, and hops?" The answer: "A frog sandwich." To the parents this was ridiculous and not very funny. Why did the children see it as so amusing? Apparently because of its incongruity. By age ten, children know that sandwiches cannot be made of live frogs. They have learned to distinguish between fact and fantasy. So, such a riddle is hilarious to them because it is an incongruous concept.

*Falling down or seeing someone fall is funny* to children (and to many adults). Seeing a person who should be upright, suddenly sprawl on his back with arms and legs in unusual positions is funny because it is unexpected and it is unusual. By the time a child knows for certain how the human being should appear, any sudden departure from that stance is apt to be seen as funny.

*Children's jokes and humor meet real needs.* One of these is to relieve the anxiety of being separated from a beloved person. Even as an infant your child enjoyed playing peek-a-boo with you. Such a game reenacted his fear of losing you, and then reassured him that you were there after all.

As children grow older they become aware of their inferior place in the world of adults. Such powerful figures as teachers, principals, policemen, and sometimes parents, can be threatening to a child who realizes how dependent he is upon them for his very security. One way he relieves his anxiety about the powerful adults in his life is to joke about them with other children. He invents names for his principal. He twists his teacher's name into combinations of syllables that other kids find funny. He draws caricatures of the adults he knows that the other children see as amusing. Their encouragement is heady stuff, and he may come to think of himself as a wit. All this is innocent school children's release in humor of what might otherwise be fearful to them.

## Should You Send Your Child to Nursery School?

Your friends and family may tell you that it is not necessary to send your child to nursery school. They may feel that it is merely a glorified baby-sitting service. They may remind you that there are other children in the neighborhood with whom your child can play. They may make you feel guilty as a mother for even suggesting that your child seems ready for nursery school experience. You know you could use the extra hours each day that your child would spend in nursery school. But that is not the main reason why you are considering giving your child this opportunity.

*Advantages of nursery school are several.* In such a setting your child would face the challenge of standing up for his rights as a member of the group. He could be helped to express his feelings without hurting other children. His nursery school teacher would be there to protect him, and the other children from too much aggression. Her supervision and direction of the children's play would assure them of getting maximum benefit from their interaction.

*Developing a sense of autonomy* within a group of children his own age is of great value to the three-to-five-year-old child. It is then that your child is ready to get a sense of himself as different from others around him. He now is ready for a healthy sense of his own powers and strengths as well as his limitations. He needs to develop a sense of responsibility for himself in order to grow on to the next stage of his development.

*A nursery school or kindergarten supplies a wide variety of materials* and equipment. It is an unusual family that can provide as much space and all the supplies for children's play that almost any good nursery program has. These range all the way from big areas for building, climbing, digging, and other large-muscle activities, to quiet-time play of various kinds. As your child plays with these varied materials, his imagination develops, He begins to take initiative in his own projects, in ways that often surprise his parents. The youngster who tags after his mother at home asking, "What can I do now, Mommy?" in a good preschool program goes purposefully to the center of his current interest and loses himself in it.

*Children's intellectual development* is encouraged in present-day preschool programs. Youngsters learn to identify letters of the alphabet, numerals, and how they are used in everyday life. Many a three-to-five-year-old spontaneously begins to print his name and to point out letters and words he knows in print. Some children have taught themselves to read before they get into first grade. To cultivate this early interest and intellectual potential, many a kindergarten now has tape recorders, typewriters, and large print children's books available. There is some question among authorities whether emphasis on specific learnings should start so early. Some children seem to be ready for it, while others are not. A good preschool provides a variety of learning opportunities, without pressure upon any one child to engage in them. It is agreed that getting children ready to read, by developing interest through trips, pets, reading aloud, talking about pictures and stories, is an important function of a preschool program.

*Children's facility with speech and language* grows rapidly in groups of their peers involved in stimulating play. They talk over what they are doing with one another. They make plans together, and evaluate their progress. Their vocabulary grows day by day as new ideas, materials, and situations present themselves. As other children and the teacher use correct words for things and functions, even the most deprived youngster outgrows his baby talk or poor language habits.

*Skilled preschool teachers assure your child* of making the most of this period of his life. Teachers of young children have been especially trained to help children grow optimally. They know how to supervise children's play so that each child has his chance to develop in his own way. They are able to protect the shy, quiet youngster from the more boisterous and the aggressive ones. They know how to pace young children's activities with a minimum of fatigue and a maximum of interest. They are warm and accepting, yet firm in setting the limits children need. Having such skilled leadership for young children is far superior to the freewheeling play of neighborhood youngsters where a child may be hurt, or ridiculed, or ignored, with no protection of a supervising adult.

One authority in early childhood education says that preschool experience is so important that he would borrow money if necessary to send his child to nursery school and kindergarten. He reminds parents that they think nothing of providing the tuition and other costs for college education. Yet a child's formative early years of learning are even more important. When your child gets a good start in his personality development during the first four or five years of his life, he has a solid foundation for his later learnings.

*Disadvantaged children's special needs* are met in preschool programs. Many youngsters from deprived neighborhoods have not learned how to speak so that others can understand them. They sometimes do not even know themselves by name. When a little child has always been referred to as "one of the younguns" his sense of personal identity has been delayed. He needs special help in preschool in learning to respond to his own name, to seeing it on his clothing hook and resting mat, and recognizing himself as a person separate from the others. He may have had few toys or play materials, and so is retarded in learning the feel and mastery of many things more fortunate youngsters have been exposed to since babyhood. Books and songs and games may not have been part of his experience at home, that now introduce him to whole new worlds of new experiences.

Many authorities in preschool children's development point out that children in deprived neighborhoods, are behind children in more affluent families. Their physical, language, mental, social, and personal growth are retarded because they lack the stimulation for optimal development. Therefore, the argument is that some public support for day care centers should be available, so that all children get off to a good start. This issue will not be settled for some time to come. But the fact remains that money spent in widespread good preschool centers is an investment in the human resources of the nation. Studies show that the greatest gains are made by children with most room for improvement.

### Selecting a Good Nursery School and Kindergarten

There are many kinds of preschool programs. Knowing what to expect of each of them is helpful in your choice of one for your child. Your community may have one or more of such programs as those listed below.

*Children's day care centers* are available in some neighborhoods to care for little children while their mothers work. They are open all day, from as early as 6:30 in the morning to 6:00 in the evening. This means that they are prepared to feed the children their meals and snacks, see that they get their naps, and supervise their play. Costs have to be kept low enough for working mothers to pay. So, food, sanitation, and safety are given top priority, and some of the "extras," such as trained preschool teachers and elaborate equipment cannot be afforded at the rates that are charged.

*Public school preschool programs are available* in some communities. Kindergartens are part of the school system in many districts now. These are open to four- and five-year-olds, who are registered in advance, as children at higher grade levels do. In some places, there is a preschool round-up before school opens for health and immunization checkups for children who will be entering kindergarten for the first time. Public school kindergartens can be as good as the local budget and personnel afford. Some are well-run, beautifully equipped, and do a fine job. Others, in less affluent school districts do the best they can with the resources they have.

*College and university demonstration preschool programs* are found in connection with many colleges of education across the country. These are essentially laboratories where future teachers of little children are being trained. Teachers in training are young, eager, and are developing their talents in the fields of their choice. These student teachers are carefully supervised by experienced members of the faculty. Such college operated preschool programs usually have excellent equipment, and programs geared to little children's readiness and interests. They are so good that in many college towns there is a long waiting list for future preschool registrations. Faculty families are given an inside chance to enroll their preschoolers, but efforts are usually made to keep places open for children from different backgrounds in the community.

*Private nursery schools and kindergartens* range from excellent to deplorable. Some have established themselves as responsible, well-run, and educationally sound programs. These may be in connection with churches, community agencies, or operated privately. They may be operating as a public service or simply as moneymaking for their owners. As a parent, you should not be taken in by flashy exteriors or attractive advertisements. You must be discriminating in what to look for in choosing a good program for your preschool child.

*What should you look for in choosing a preschool* for your child? Your friends and neighbors probably will recommend the nursery school or kindergarten that they have found good for their children. You will want to look into these for yourself before registering your child. Start with the one(s) closest to you, for convenience sake. But do not let ease of transportation overly influence you. It could be that a facility several blocks away is much superior to the handier one. Drop into those in which you are interested by appointment or unannounced. Look for such physical features as low furniture, toilets, wash bowls, hooks and doorknobs the children can reach, plenty of light and air, adequate play space inside and outside, safeguards for the children's safety, and the equipment available for their play.

*Watch the teacher especially* to make sure that she is warm and relaxed with the children. When you see her ridicule or shame a child, for whatever reason, write that preschool off. If she remains inobtrusive, letting the children be themselves most of the time, and quietly guiding their play, she merits your support. A good preschool is a happy place with just enough adult supervision to give all the children opportunity to develop in their own way. It offers a wide variety of experiences, materials, and activities with active and quiet times alternating through the day. It is geared to the childrens' developmental level, and is primarily concerned with their growth as persons.

*Cooperative nursery schools* and parent-child centers are those in which the children, their mothers, and sometimes their fathers are all involved actively in the school day. Mothers take turns in being on duty, under the supervision of a trained head teacher. Fathers may build equipment, help paint and fix furnishings, and when possible take their turns with the children, too. These have the advantages of being less costly, since the parents take the place of some employed workers. More important, the mothers and fathers learn along with their children, through the many activities that are undertaken. There is no substitute for seeing your child interact with other children in a preschool setting. You learn to appreciate your youngster's strengths and weakness when we get to know a number of children of his age. Of course, you are careful not to compare him with any others, especially to his face. Although you may tell him at bedtime how pleased you were to see him play nicely with other children.

As you take your turn in the parent-child center, you learn many of the experienced teacher's methods in guiding children's play that are of immense help in your own home. You discover how futile scolding is. You see for yourself that ignoring "show off" efforts tends to decrease them. Smiling at children's "good" conduct reinforces it for the child in question, and some of the others who have witnessed your approval. You recognize that every child from time to time comes for reassurance, and that it is all right to take an unhappy child on your lap, cuddle him or her a while, or let him sit very close to you until he is ready to move off on his own.

### Handling First-Day Clinging and Tears

Your three-year-old is not "being a baby" if he clings to you and cries as you leave him at his nursery school the first time. Some separation anxiety is to be expected on the part of most if not all nursery-school-age children the first time they see mother about to leave them in a strange group of children, in a strange place, with a teacher who is not familiar.

Andy's mother coped comfortably with his tears on his first day of nursery school. She took him inside the door of the room where the children were gathering. She introduced him to the teacher, who held out her hand for Andy's. Andy drew back to his mother and clung to her skirts. She sat down where she was, and assured Andy that she would stay as long as he wanted her to. After a few minutes, he moved away far enough to begin playing with a toy fire engine. She smiled at him, and asked if it was all right for her to leave now and do the shopping. His lip quivered, and she told him she would come right back for him, and that they would take the groceries home together, a task he always enjoyed. He assented to her leaving, but by the time she had reached the door, he ran to her in tears. She took him on her lap and told him it was all right; she could stay, there was no hurry. She held him until he moved off again to see the pictures and listen to a story the teacher was reading the other children. From time to time, he glanced anxiously back to his mother to make sure she was still there. She stayed that whole first morning, quietly in the background where he could see her The second morning, he needed her there only the first half-hour. The third morning he told her as they approached the nursery school door, that she could go do the shopping now, and he would help her put the groceries away when they went home together. By not forcing the issue of her abrupt separation from him, he was able to take the initiative himself, when he was ready.

Some nursery school and kindergarten teachers prefer to handle children's separation anxiety themselves. You will be wise to check with your child's teacher before enrolling him to find out her policy on parents' remaining in the room until their children are ready to be left there alone. Just remember that all little children have some emotional discomfort the first time their mothers leave them. Those whose parents have prepared them for preschool are more at ease than those who have not grown accustomed to adapting to new situations and persons.

### Preparing Your Child for Preschool

You prepare your child for his first group experiences, by gradually exposing him to new places and persons. You may have let him stay overnight with his grandparents or other relatives from time to time. He may have learned to enjoy visiting in a neighborhood child's home for a meal, a party, or an evening while his parents are away. He probably has gone to the little children's department of Sunday School where he has learned that even though you leave, you will come back for him. He likes to tell you about it when it is over, and so what he has done becomes a family experience. All this makes him feel like a "big boy," or girl, as a participating member of the family.

*Your child needs help in learning to manage his own clothing* without help before he goes to preschool. He should be able to indicate his needs clearly so as to minimize the "accidents" that can be embarrassing to a little child. If he has any special problems, these can be discussed with his teacher before he is left the first time. You will want to confer with your child's teacher from time to time so that you and she together can plan for your child's progress. There is much that she can tell you about how he gets along with other children and what he seems to especially enjoy. You can tell her a great deal about him that will help her as his first teacher.

Your child no doubt will want to tell you about his day in

nursery or kindergarten. You will learn to listen, not only to his accounts of what happened, and what he did, but especially to how he felt about it. The feelings his reports reflect can tell you a great deal about his inner response to the preschool experience.

*Flights of fantasy that punctuate your child's reports* need not be taken seriously. Listen attentively to the story of the lion that came into the yard while he was playing. Ask him how he felt about it. Express interest in what he did to or with the lion. Mildly remind him that the only lions in your community are at the zoo, but do not make a fuss about it. It is not necessary to scold him for lying. His imagination is growing fast these days, and he yet has to learn to distinguish between reality and fantasy.

Watch for tales about some other child's misbehavior. At this age, a little youngster is trying hard to live up to your expectations of being good, and of avoiding what he knows is bad. One way of doing this is to describe what he himself wanted to do, but didn't, as actually being done by some imaginary playmate. This scapegoat function of his made-up companions is important to him, and need not alarm you unduly. Agree with him that such misbehavior as he is describing is bad. By all means avoid challenging him on the existence of the make-believe culprit. When he can get along without the imaginary wrongdoer, he will stop talking about him on his own.

From now on, your child will take you out into the community in ever-widening circles. Before long you will be involved in PTA, parents' church groups, summer camp, sports, trips, and a wide variety of experiences you never would have were it not for your children's introduction of you to them. You will come to be known as "Mary's mother," or "Charlie's father" rather than as by your own name in some circles. Your new identity as a parent will be disturbing or satisfying depending on how freely you give yourself to going out to others with your children.

# 8. SEEING OTHERS THROUGH CHILDREN'S EYES

Arthur talked a great deal about his friend, Lee, in kindergarten. The day that Arthur's mother visited kindergarten, she made a point of getting acquainted with her son's best friends. That afternoon when Arthur returned home from kindergarten and was having his fruit juice with his mother, she asked, "Isn't your friend, Lee, Japanese?" Arthur's reply was, "I don't know, I'll ask him."

Your child sees others at first through the views you as parents provide. Because Arthur's parents had not put much emphasis on racial differences, Arthur had not even noticed that his kindergarten friend was Asian. Studies show that usually by the age of five children make black-white distinctions. By this age too, they have picked up the stereotypes of their and others' racial background. These are funneled through family attitudes and feelings about brotherhood or prejudice.

## Children's Best Friends

Children usually choose their best friends from among their own social, religious, and racial groups. One reason for this is that similar families tend to cluster in neighborhoods, where children have access largely to their "own kind of people." One other reason is the subtle, but powerful, pressures upon children to associate with other children like themselves. Other children expect friends to be like one another in conspicuous ways. Many parents let their children know that they prefer them to be friendly with children from homes like theirs. They welcome "nice little boys and girls" from families they know; and are less enthusiastic about children from obviously different backgrounds.

*Your child follows your example* in choosing his friends. If your family is broad in its interests and social life, your child will be too. Children of United Nations' staff are daily exposed to other children from many other countries around the world. They go to school together. Their parents know one another both in work and social situations. They become familiar with children of many races and nationalities as they grow up. Quite different is the experience of children growing up in a small, homogeneous community with little opportunity of meeting and knowing people unlike themselves.

*Schoolchildren follow the leader* in their neighborhood. Studies show that youngsters between five and twelve tend to admire, and to follow, the leaders whom other children prefer. There is a strong tendency among school children to look up to the boy or girl whom their classmates admire. They like to be seen with these leaders. When possible, they want to be friends with them.

*Leaders among children are usually brighter* than their followers. They are usually better students and generally are a good example. Parents' worry about the bad influence of the youngsters their children admire is usually unfounded. Of course, there are unfortunate children whose daring exploits excite their classmates. But on the whole, your child is not likely to be overly drawn to classmates who are not a good influence on him. When you have a question about some child whom your son or daughter is friendly with, it may be wise to soft-pedal your concern until you have become acquainted with the child yourself. Perhaps, as you see your child in association with the one you question, you will see what it is that the friendship means.

*Shared interests bring good friends together.* As your child develops skills, they take him out to others who share these interests. Your son learns to pitch and catch a ball, and he is accepted by the other boys who play baseball. Your daughter swims well and is a part of the group who share aquatic interests. It is the youngster who can do things who gets to know other children with similar interests. The tendency is for children who are athletically inclined to find their friends among those who enjoy sports. There is a strong likelihood that musically talented children make friends with others who play in the little musicales, children's bands, sing in the junior choirs, as tone-deaf children do not. This is true of adults, too, of course. Church-oriented families make their friends among religious people. Golfers' friends are often other golfers. It is persons' interests that take them out to others at every age—young child or adult.

## Being Masculine or Feminine

Boys and girls feel strongly about being masculine or feminine A schoolboy who plays with girls is apt to be made fun of by the other fellows. If he shows an interest in feminine activities, that labels him as "Sissy," in many communities. So, too, with a girl's interest in masculine pursuits. The grade-school girl who climbs trees, or plays sand-lot baseball may be known as a tomboy in the neighborhood. These lines are not so clearly drawn now as they once were, but they are present in children's world nevertheless. A boy is expected to be "all-boy." A girl is expected to be "a little lady." What each may and may not do is fairly clear to most children of both sexes by their grade school years.

*Boys and girls play differently.* More boys than girls play with transportation toys (cars, trucks, airplanes, spaceships), with mechanical and building materials (tool sets, erector sets, etc.), and participate in sports of many kinds. Girls' activities as seen by both boys and girls are in the areas of playing house, playing school, dressing up, and working at art projects of various kinds.

A child of three already knows whether he is a boy or a girl. He, or she, knows a great deal about what is appropriate behavior for members of his own and the other sex. By the fifth grade, schoolchildren see boys as typically not afraid of anything, liking to show off, being noisy, bossy, and liking to tease. Feminine behavior is seen by fifth-graders as doing what the teacher says, liking to act grown up, being polite, careful not to hurt other people's feelings, and being easily embarrassed. Such sharp differences between masculine and feminine behavior are fading in recent years, but they are by no means all gone in children's minds, or in their families.

*You teach your child his sex role.* When your baby was born, you probably dressed your little girl in pink and your boy in blue. Your friends asked the sex of your baby before bringing the appropriate color in toys, clothing, and blankets. You may have dodged the issue by putting your baby in yellow, or some other pastel color. But it seemed "right" to connect blue with boys, and pink with girls. So too with style of clothes. Baby boys look "cute" in blue jeans. Little girls are "darling" in frilly, fluffy clothes. If you yourself do not make such distinctions, one of the baby's grandmothers or other relatives will. It is a powerful pressure to buck, even by a "sexually liberated" household.

*You played with your baby boy differently* than you did with your infant daughter. Without realizing it, fathers and mothers handle their boys more boisterously than they do their girls. They expect their sons to be "little men" and to take their bumps without crying. Little girls are cuddled and comforted, and expected to cry when they are hurt. Fathers are more gentle with their little daughters than with their sons. They talk more softly to them; they stroke their shiny hair and tell them how beautiful they are, as they rarely do with their sons. Fathers and their little daughters are often flirtatious with each other, quite spontaneously.

Fathers and mothers unconsciously reward their sons for being masculine, and their daughters for their feminine conduct. When a little girl uses her mother's lipstick or eye make-up, her parents laugh and feel it is cute. If their young son does the same thing, they are worried, scold him, and make him wash it off at once. It is all right for a little boy to follow his father into the bathroom, and watch his father shave, while making pretend-shaving motions himself. Many a father would feel less inclined to have his small daughter join him in his shaving. These are early lessons in masculinity and femininity that every family teaches in its own way—by rewarding what they like and frowning upon the conduct they sense is inappropriate for a child of one sex or the other.

*Children learn to be masculine or feminine by identifying* with the parent of their own sex. Little girls follow their mother around the house, helping set the table, make the beds, sewing, cleaning, and caring for others. They talk over their toy telephones in the same inflections they hear their mothers using in their conversations. They dress up in their mother's clothing and pretend to go on shopping trips, to give tea parties, and act out the life they see their mothers living. A boy as young as two or three typically puts on his father's hat, carries his briefcase or lunch pail, and mimics the grown man's stance and walk as much as his chubby legs will allow. Older boys go with their fathers, and other male relatives to ball games, and all-men affairs where they further imitate masculine behavior. By the time a child goes to school, he, or she, has already practiced being a man or a woman in hundreds of hours of play. Other models of masculinity and femininity among relatives and friends, on television and in reading, further help a child know what is expected both of boys and of girls.

## Your Children's Grandparents

Your children may enjoy their grandparents, as many youngsters do. Studies find that grandmothers are often close confidantes of their grandchildren from babyhood on through the teen years. Your mother quite possibly was the person who came to be with you when your baby was born. She stayed on to help get the new baby and mother settled in before returning to her own home. You may have been glad to have her come and happy to have her leave so that you could be alone with your baby those first precious weeks.

*Three-generation-studies of American families* find that it is to grandparents that young families turn for help when they need it. This may be of the personal service sort such as helping with the new baby, baby-sitting, and being available when sickness or accidents come. It often is in the form of financial help with the big expenses of young families: the down-payment on the car, your first house, medical costs, and special trips and vacations. It is not unusual for children's grandparents to maintain a summer cottage to which their grandchildren and their parents come for their family holidays.

*Grandparents are of many kinds.* Some are warm and welcome in your home. Others are more difficult to get along with. Research finds that three out of five grandmothers and grandfathers enjoy their roles as grandparents. Some enjoy playing with their grandchildren. They take them on excursions, to ball games, the zoo, and the park. They invite their grandchildren from early ages to spend the night in their home, and often to stay for a week or more at a time. This gives the youngster a home away from home, where they are loved and cared for, and seen as "special people."

*Your children probably love their grandparents* in very special ways. They enjoy one another without the heavy responsibility that children have in measuring up to their parents' expectations. They frolic with fun-loving grandparents, and learn to be considerate of those who are ill or tired or otherwise indisposed. They look forward to their grandparents' remembering their birthdays and other special occasions. They print their first letters to their favorite grandparent, and spend hours making some little gift to please him, or her.

You foster a mutually pleasant relationship between your parents and your children when you are careful not to criticize one or the other unduly. There will be times, perhaps, when your mother may seem too intrusive in her efforts to be helpful. If you can appreciate what she is trying to do without openly accusing her of meddling, the intergenerational relationships in your family will benefit from your consideration. Similarly, you can bring up your children to be thoughtful of their grandparents. They can be taught to respect them from an early age. Their gratitude for favors and gifts expressed in immediate thank-you's is appreciated. This will take a little persuasion on your part as parents, at first. Courtesies do not come easily, but are worth working for with your children.

## Who's Good? What's Bad?

You guide your child to choose to do the right thing in many situations while he or she is growing up. By the time your youngster is out of babyhood, he or she is beginning to know what you expect of him. When he does something well, you smile at him, praise him, and let him know that you are pleased. You may tell him outright that he is a big boy when he acts so well. You let your little girl know how pleased you are with the way she is behaving.

*Parents discourage disapproved conduct* with a frown, or other expression of their disappointment. Long before your child can talk he can understand what you mean when you say: "That was a naughty thing to do. Mother does not like you to be mean to the dog." You are careful to label the behavior bad, and reassure your child that you expect him to be a good boy. When he is acting up, your ignoring his behavior has the effect of discouraging it as an attention-getting device.

*Little children scold themselves* for misconduct as soon as they can talk. They remind themselves of their parents' teaching by repeating "No-no," as they are about to do something that is forbidden. In this way your child puts your approval or disapproval inside himself. In time it becomes his conscience, that still small voice that guides him as you have. A child feels guilty when he has done something wrong; he says to himself, "I should not have done that." If you have made it easy for him to tell you what has happened, he can confess his mistake and be relieved of the guilty feeling that can be so burdensome.

*Your child expects you to be firm and consistent.* He is confused when you are strict at one time and permissive at others. When he has done something wrong, he expects you to join him in disapproving the misbehavior. Your punishment need not be severe. Letting him know, in no uncertain terms, that such things are wrong, and that you expect more of your child than that is usually enough. What you consider right or wrong is an expression of your values and beliefs as parents. You are fortunate if you both can agree on the general principles of good character. When parents disagree on what is right and what is wrong, it makes it that much harder for children to know what is right. They usually follow the parent to whom they feel closest. But this can be a strain on their relationship with the other parent.

## Religious Education of Your Child

Your child's religious education began when he was born. By coming into your family, he immediately shared your religious place in the community. His coming was probably noted in your church. Your pastor no doubt called to welcome this new little member of the congregation. Friends and neighbors saw this new baby as belonging to your faith, and expected him or her to grow up in your church.

*Your religious practices in the family* gave your child concrete expression of religious living long before he or she was big enough to take to Sunday School. Saying grace at meals, joining in family prayers, going to church and Sunday School on Sundays, participating in church activities through the week, seeing money dropped into special collection boxes on the family table, or in a religious service, are the kinds of family practices that help a child place himself as a child of God from his earliest years.

*Church nurseries and Sunday School* are important to a child. They take him into a climate of reverence. He sees others in corporate worship, and soon joins in with bowed head and folded hands. He enjoys the religious hymns and sings them with gusto as soon as he is able to carry a tune. Sometimes he tries before he has the words straight or the music on key. If he is not laughed at for his efforts to participate, he will continue to try. He learns to give his pennies in the collection, and to share with others in many ways.

*Bible stories and religious drama* give a child a sense of history even before he understands it fully. He feels rooted in something that has been going on a long time before he was born. He senses that there is something bigger than he is, and that stretches both forward and backward through time. Knowing Bible verses and passages, helps a child know his religious heritage. He shares a common culture with other members of his family's faith. He learns to revere the Bible as God's word, as revealed to the great founders of his faith.

*Nature appreciation is an important part* of a child's religious education. He comes to delight in "all things bright and beautiful," and to rejoice in the wonders of God's world. To the truly religious person, who has become atune to the miracles in nature, every walk can be a worship experience. You parents lead your child into the world around them, and he shares with you as well as with his religious teachers the attitudes and the feelings that are yours. If an insect your child brings to you is received as "just a bug, throw it away," his appreciation of the amazing variety of life will be that much diminished. When you join with your child in exploring the yard, the park, and the beach for the wonders they hold, you revitalize your religious awareness, as you help him develop his.

*Answering children's religious questions* is a real challenge to parents. A little child can ask questions that have baffled philosophers for centuries. His searching need to know takes him, and you, into deep waters where your faith is tested. Your ability to put your beliefs into words is of great help to your child and it may be a way in which you clarify some of your own religious concepts.

You are wise to do the best you can in responding to your child's questions, at the time. When you dodge them or suggest that he ask his Sunday School teacher, you are giving your child the impression that you are not sure of your own ground. You will not find it hard to be humble about many of your child's queries. But you should attempt to reply.

The way you answer your child's questions depends upon your own beliefs and practices as parents. When he asks you why God doesn't give him what he has prayed for, you have an opportunity to talk over what prayer is, and what it is not, as you see it. When your child asks you what God looks like, you have the challenge of describing him in words a child can understand. At the first Christmas season when he wonders how Santa Claus got into the birth of the Christ child celebration, yours is the task of helping him see the difference between the sacred and the secular aspects of religious holidays like Christmas and Easter.

When you are baffled as to how best to respond to your child's recurrent questions, you can get help with them. You can say to your youngster, "That is a good question, dear, let's find out more about it." This accepts the question, and gives you time to consult your pastor, or the child's Sunday School teacher, or to get a book from the library on answering children's questions.

*Life and death are religious matters.* These are among the most difficult for adults to deal with, because they involve the very depths of being. When your child comes home from singing Christmas carols to ask, "What is a virgin?" you are expected to answer. What you say and how you say it make a difference not only in your child's religious education, but his sex education as well. Your child's first experience with death is difficult for him and for you. His beloved grandfather dies, and he wants to know where he has gone and when he will see him again. He probably asks what it means to die—a question many adults grapple with for years.

*Emphasizing virtues is part of religious education.* As your child goes with you to Sunday School and church, he gets a renewed emphasis of the virtues you as parents have been trying to instill in him. He is expected to give, as adults do, in the collection plate, the Salvation Army kettle at holiday time, and to various causes that you and he are expected to support. When this giving is something that is not only expected but rewarded as a good thing to do by you and others, he gets satisfaction in it. This free giving of what he has continues later as he becomes older, until it is in time a lifelong habit. Religious people generally are more generous than the nonchurched.

A little child knows something of the meaning of compassion. He hurts when another child is abused. He cries when he sees his pet injured. These feelings of sorrow in another creature's plight are emphasized both in a good home and in religious settings. His ability to empathize with another's distress grows as he grows, until in time he can feel with those whom he has not met, and wants to help many whose distress he knows only through hearsay.

Wanting to help is a religious virtue that is caught as much as taught. Your child sees you going out on missions of mercy, and he wants to help too. He hears some dire need discussed at church or at home, and his tendency is to follow the example he is given. Parents who are afraid of being involved should not be surprised to find that their children hold back from trying to help also. Those who serve others freely tend to bring up their children with the same willingness to help in any way they can. Your child's desire to give, to share, and to help grows as he learns what it means to love in unselfish ways.

## Love Is a Lifelong Process

Love is not easy to define. It comes in so many forms, for so many persons. Generally, it includes the kind of attachment that is durable, warm, and full of mutual caring and concern for one another. This kind of love your child learns first in his relationship with you parents during the formative years of his life as a little child.

*Your child's first love was with his mother.* This attachment was strong and deep. Both mother and baby enjoyed their close association as she fed and changed, bathed and dressed him. He needed her and he knew it. She was needed and she enjoyed this new stage in her development as a woman. This first loving relationship was the foundation for all other loves to come. In time, father, siblings, other relatives, friends, and God himself came to be loved each in their own way, by the child who was learning to go out to others with affection.

Your little boy saw his mother as his first sweetheart. Somewhere around his third birthday, he let you know that he wanted her for his wife. He became jealous of his father, may even have told him to "Go away, I want Mommy to sleep with me." When his parents take this in stride, the little boy learns that he cannot marry his mother, she already is wed to his father. He sees his father as big and strong and powerful. He looks to him for discipline and punishment when he goes astray. So, during the time he is jealous of his father, he may have dreams and nightmares of some avenging monster (lions, tigers, bears) who come after him. This happens to many little boys as they work through their romantic love feelings for their mother and their jealousy of their father.

*When you parents are understanding,* do not ridicule but comfort and reassure him, you help him grow through this intense love tangle to the next stage of his emotional development. He turns to identifying with his father, and tries to be just like him in many ways. Meanwhile he holds deep within himself the image of his mother as the kind of woman he will someday marry when he becomes a man. This is the truth behind the song, "I want a girl just like the girl who married dear old dad."

*Your daughter's love shifted from her mother* to her father when she was three years of age more or less. The little girl saw her father as her first sweetheart (he may have called her that). She did what she could to take care of him, as she saw her mother doing. Her identification with her mother sent her about the house cleaning and washing and cooking and being helpful to others, as her mother did. She was delighted when her mother had to leave for awhile, telling her that she was now the lady of the house. This gave her a chance to show her father what a fine little sweetheart she was. Because she felt jealous of her mother, she may have feared that her mother would take revenge and punish her for trying to take her husband away from her. So, it is not unusual for a little girl between three and six years of age to have bad dreams of witches and who are thinly disguised Mother out to get her. With reassurance and clear understanding that Father and Mother are lovers as she could never be, the little girl accepts the fact that she must grow up and find a man of her own—like her father!

This first family romance is played out in many ways in many houses. It is the stuff of life and love. It is not to be ridiculed, or shamed, or belittled. The little boy or girl must be let down easy; they must be led to see the facts through their fantasy. They are helped most by parents whose marriage is firm and strong. They need most mothers and fathers who have learned to love widely and deeply. Such families provide the models of caring for others that a child can build upon throughout his lifetime.

# 9. BECOMING RESPONSIBLE AT HOME AND SCHOOL

Children first learn to be responsible in the family. Responsibility broadens both for them and their parents as they begin their school experience. Fathers and mothers do what they can to instill in their children a sense of responsibility through the years. Children tend to follow the patterns of responsibility they have been taught in the family.

### Your Child's Responsibility for His Appearance

Many a youngster begins to be interested in how he or she looks as a preschooler. A three-year-old girl can make a big fuss about which outfit she wears. A boy not much older insists upon wearing one particular pair of shoes until they are worn-out, while other pairs, much nicer sit unused in his closet. This is the time for parents to recognize that the youngster is demonstrating his readiness to help choose his own clothing.

*Choosing clothes for the day* can begin with simple choices at an early age. Mother may bring out a blue outfit and a red one, and ask the child which he, or she, wants to wear that day. Letting the little boy or girl participate in the choice of the day's clothing helps develop in him an interest in his appearance, and it gives him an opportunity to learn to make choices about what he will wear.

*Clothing appropriate to the occasion* must be a joint decision for parent and child. Your youngster knows what the other kids are wearing, often better than do you. On the other hand, parents are aware of what is appropriate for a particular situation better than a child can. For instance, completely washable, sturdy fabrics are best for an outing where grass stains, dirt, and food spots are to be expected. "Good clothes" for church, Sunday School, and parties should be nice enough to satisfy the expectations of the parents and other adults who will be seeing your children. Otherwise, you are made to feel that somehow you have neglected your child's appearance.

*Taking weather into consideration* is important in selecting clothes for a particular day. When the temperature plummets, a child should have clothing warm enough to protect him from chilling. This can be a struggle in your family, unless you enlist the help of some objective authority, in the decision. One family we know, has established the practice of checking the reading on the outdoor thermometer before settling on the clothing for a given day. Another sends the child to check the local weather report on television or radio before he dresses himself. In most communities one can call a specified telephone number for the local weather report. Employing the assistance of such an authoritative source can avoid many an argument about how cold it is, or what the prediction is for the hours ahead.

*Care of clothing is a family concern.* Some families make a practice of hanging up the clothes that will be worn again, immediately upon removing them. This requires hooks or rods low enough for a little child to reach with ease. It calls for his parents' encouragement by praise, example, and consistent expectation of the habit of keeping clothing hung up.

Soiled clothing left where a child has peeled it off can become a messy habit, that can be avoided by early training. When father and mother regularly put their soiled garments in hamper or washer, their children can be expected to follow their example. If the soiled clothing receptacle is convenient to the bedrooms, children can be taught from early ages to use it as soon as the dirty garments are taken off. One mother we know, has trained her family to turn all pockets inside out as their garments are put in the dirty clothes hamper. This protects their treasures, and saves her time in doing the family laundry.

*Dirty necks, ears, and hands* become an issue in many a family. Cleanliness is not a value to a busy youngster. He, or she, is much too involved in the project of the moment to waste time in washing. So, the tendency is to slip out of the cleaning-up procedures that are expected in the hope that no one will notice. One child psychologist says that any boy under the age of ten who voluntarily washes his hands before coming to the table loves his mother!

Should you send him back to clean up when your son comes to meal unwashed? What you do, depends of course on how you feel about it. There is some danger of salmonella infection and other health hazards from eating with dirty hands. But these dangers can be exaggerated by overly-zealous parents. Your own sensibilities determine how fussy you are about your youngster's appearance at the family table. One father put the problem well when he told his boy: "Son, you are old enough now to make your own decisions about your appearance, but I find it hard to swallow my food with you looking like something the cat dragged in. So, either clean yourself up before coming to meals in this house, or arrange to eat when I'll not have to see you." The boy grinned sheepishly, replied: "OK, Dad, if that's the way you feel, I'll watch it."

*Hair care has become an issue in many families.* Boys, as well as girls, tend to prefer their hair longer than was in fashion some years ago. Trends in hair length shift with the styles and require consideration on the part of family members of both generations. Parents who recognize that their children want to appear in step with their own generation do not put up too much resistance to their youngsters' wishes in hair length and style. After all, it is not a big deal that endangers the child one way or another. When he, or she, wants to change his hair style, it can be done with little expenditure of time and money.

Keeping hair clean and manageable is another matter. A youngster's hair that is allowed to grow thick and matted with dirt is unsightly, smelly, and an indication of parental neglect, in the eyes of many an adult. Therefore, some standards for cleanliness have to be established in the family. How often should hair be washed? When it needs it, is the simplest answer. It depends upon how hot the weather and how dirty and sweaty the youngster has become. It is greatly influenced by the child's interest in his appearance. Many a family has despaired of ever getting their son to shampoo his head and then finds him often wet-headed when some little girl has dropped a soft hint in this direction.

Parents help their children with hair care when they supply mild shampoo materials that are safe and easy to use when the child bathes or showers. At times a gentle reminder with the reason given for being particularly well-groomed may be in order. "Remember, we are going to the church party tonight, and so should all be bathed, shampooed, and dressed in time to get there when the food is served." This built-in motivation is enough for many a child, who might otherwise resist cutting short playtime to bathe and shampoo. The general principle is for the child to assume as much responsibility for his appearance as he can, with his parents the back-up encouragers and facilitators of his personal grooming and care.

### Cluttered Room and Strewn Toys—Whose Responsibility?

Families differ widely in how much clutter they allow their members. In some homes, things are dropped when they were used, and no one takes much responsibility for keeping the place in order. In other families, there is a strict·pick-up policy in which everyone is expected to replace any and all objects as soon as they have been used. Some families let things accumulate and then have a cleanup time when everyone pitches in and helps straighten the place; in others even periodic housecleaning is neglected.

*Some projects cannot but clutter,* at least for awhile. A school boy building a model plane must leave it out until he can finish it. It is unreasonable to expect him to put it neatly away until the paint has dried. Father and son building a boat in backyard or basement will have to clutter the place for weeks. Teenagers remodelling a car may have parts strewn about for days. Mother's sewing is not easy to put away each time she is called away from it for some other activity. So, pick-up policies must be flexible in order to work at all.

*Children habitually irresponsible* in dropping their belongings anywhere can be guided toward neater habits. Scolding, fussing, and nagging are negative efforts that usually fall on deaf ears. But making a game of keeping things in order appeals to some children, some of the time. One mother has developed a "lost and found" service for her family. Whenever she finds something out of place, she puts it in her lost and found chest for reclaiming by its owner. This keeps the house fairly neat, and prepares the children for what to expect in school and other public places with things that are left where they do not belong.

*Cleaning up your child's room* can be a mutual responsibility—yours and his. At times his clutter becomes so discouraging that he is overwhelmed with it. Then it is a temptation for Mother to assume control, barge into the child's room with determination, and take over completely. If she is expecting friends in, she may prefer to clean up her child's room herself to having a struggle with him to do it. There is another possibility that works at times. Mother and son, or daughter, agree that it is time to clean up the place. The youngster starts to pick up his things and then dawdles, stalls, or otherwise seems to lose interest in what he has started to do.

Instead of either fussing at him to finish the job, or chasing him out and taking over herself, one mother we knew came to the door of the child's room, in an attitude of helpfulness. She asked, "Is there anything you would like me to do to help you?" The daughter in relief said, "Oh, Mother, would you?" At this the mother did not take the responsibility from her daughter, but responded with, "All right, what do you want me to do first?" She undertook the particular part of the straightening project that her daughter indicated, and then waited for the girl to assign her the next. In this way, the girl was not relieved of her primary responsibility for her own room, while her mother helped her out of a mess too great to straighten all alone.

### Getting Ready for School on Time

When your child starts to school, you and he face the joint responsibility of getting him ready on time. This has to be a mutual responsibility at least for awhile. Few children are ready by age five or six to be completely able to get themselves off to school in the morning without adult help.

*Morning routines call for complicated scheduling and timing.* In most families there is a morning rush as all the family members get ready for their day. In a family where both mother and father work, and the children must be readied for school, this can be an especially hectic time in the family day. Everyone must get into and out of the bathroom with time enough to toilet, wash, brush teeth, and comb hair. Pressure on the one or two bathroom home can be relieved by providing grooming and hair care facilities in the individual bedroom, rather than in the family bathroom. Developing a schedule in which those who have to leave earliest get the first use of the bathroom helps. Being flexible enough to allow for early and late risers in the morning timing of the use of joint facilities makes for smooth scheduling.

Parents are wise to insist that their children have an adequate breakfast before leaving for school. This is best assured when the family breakfasts together. Time can be allowed not only for eating the meal, but for discussing the day's plans, and for the quiet family meditation and prayer that many families find indispensable. This may mean arising fifteen or twenty minutes earlier than would be necessary for the hurried individual snatching of something to eat before leaving for the day. It can be a good investment of time in terms of the family spirit and poise.

*Collecting things for the day ahead* can be a major undertaking for your schoolchild. Books and other school materials must be found and readied for the day. Lunch or lunch money must be prepared and pocketed. Special materials for projects ahead have to be gathered, often by both child and parents. Schoolchildren have been known to forget some important request made by the school to the parents until the last minute. One second-grader forgot to tell his mother that he needed to take a dozen cupcakes for a special birthday party his class was giving their teacher, until the morning they were due. Fortunately, she had a mix on hand and was able to have them ready when he left, but it wasn't easy!

*The mother with one or more lunches to pack* each day can ease the morning pressure by preparing some of the things the night before for assembling the last minute. Carrots can be scraped and cut for carrot sticks, apples or other fruit can be washed and refrigerated the night before. Even sandwiches can be made, bagged, and put in the freezer ahead of the time they will be needed. They will thaw between the time they are put in the child's lunch bag and the time he eats them. Puddings and juicy fruits can be packed in covered plastic dishes, and refrigerated until time to be assembled in the morning. Such shortcuts ease the strain on a busy mother and allows her more time with her children before they start out for their day.

There are several practices that help a schoolchild and his family collect the things that will be needed for the school day. One is to be on hand to ask the child when he returns from school in the afternoon what projects are due the next day. While mother and son, or daughter, are having their after-school snack together, she can inquire about what's up for the next day. This may help the youngster remember the cupcakes, or special things that may be required. Leaving things out and ready the night before relieves some of the morning pressure.

Children can be taught to get the clothes they are going to wear the following day laid out before they go to bed. They can be helped to collect their schoolbooks and materials as soon as they have finished their homework. Milk money can be put into the pocket of the garment to be worn. Such things help a child assume responsibility for collecting his things without parents having to step in and do things for him. The important thing to remember is that you are not only readying your child for school, you are getting him ready to take care of himself in life. The sooner he begins to be responsible for himself, the easier it will be for him, and for you to enjoy one another as persons.

## Your Child and His Money

Money is a part of your child's experience from the time he is given his first birthday dollar, or takes something for the Sunday School collection. You, and he, cannot avoid the question of his use of money, now or through the years. Right now, while your children are with you, they are learning the ways with money that become central in their use of it as future adults.

*Your child has many needs for money.* He needs small amounts of cash for regular and special school projects: collective gifts for the teacher, money for the milk or juice he consumes in school, trips his class is about to take, and the special collections his class make for worthy projects in which he is expected to participate. He has to have money for Sunday School, church, and the appeals made upon children for contributions from time to time. He wants enough money to be able to get birthday gifts for you and other members of the family. His needs for money increase as Valentine's Day, Christmas, and other holidays approach so that he may participate in the spirit and celebration of the season. He has personal projects and interests that require monetary support. You can dole out what he needs at each time, or you can put him on an allowance, or both.

*When is your child ready for an allowance?* In general, your child is ready for a regular allowance as soon as he has predictable needs for which he is responsible. Usually this is soon after he starts going to school, when he, and you, know what his weekly costs will be, most of the time. His allowance can start on a weekly basis, or for shorter intervals if he has difficulty hanging on to his money until it is needed.

*How large should your child's allowance be?* An allowance should cover your child's predictable expenses, as closely as he and you can estimate them. When you give him too much, he may have problems with other children exploiting him unduly. If he gets too little money, he is too often embarrassed in being the only child who cannot carry his responsibility for the things he needs.

*Special needs arise from time to time* that require money beyond a child's allotted amount. These needs can be negotiated as they arise, without too much of a fuss made about his not being able to carry them out of his allowance. The situation is clarified when you and he have agreed on just what the allowance is to cover. Then, when he has expenses for which he lacks the money, it is easy to determine whether they should have been planned for out of his allowance.

*Meeting your child's deficits* is a practical as well as a philosophical question. It may be a matter of principle to you as parents to make your child responsible for keeping within his allowance. This is wise as long as your policy is flexible enough to allow for the contingencies that arise from time to time. It is a mistake to be so rigid that your child becomes discouraged about using his allowance. It is unfortunate to create the impression that your child does not have to keep within his allowance, because you parents will always bail him out when he overspends his money. The happy medium is for you to be available as back-up resources, while expecting your child to assume responsibility for keeping within his budgeted allowance most of the time.

*Taking money that does not belong to him* is a common problem for many a child. Gene came home from first grade with a note from the teacher pinned to his shirt. His mother greeted him, read the note, which read,

You will want to know that Gene took a nickel of the class milk money from my desk, this morning. I said nothing to him about it, knowing that you would want to handle the situation yourself. Sincerely,

Miss _____, first-grade teacher

Gene's mother waited until her son had finished his juice, and then said, quietly, "Son, it looks as though you and I have a problem." He looked a bit sheepish but listened as she read him his teacher's note. Then she asked him, "What do you think we can do about this?" She did not accuse him of stealing. She did not tell him that he should be punished. She did not criticize the teacher for not dealing with the problem in class where it happened. She simply put the responsibility on her six-year-old for him to suggest a solution to the problem.

Gene's first reaction was to deny the teacher's report. His mother replied that since his teacher said that he had taken the nickel, they still had to do something about it. The boy then attacked his teacher as being "a snitcher" and a "tattle-tale;" conduct he had heard his mother disapprove on other occasions when he had told on some other child for wrongdoing. His mother stood firmly this time, however, by saying that it was the teacher's job to account for the class milk money, and to help her children learn to respect others' property.

Gene's mother sat quietly beside him while he explored other ways out of his discomfort. He finally brightened and suggested that he take five cents from his piggy bank, and put it back on the teacher's desk. His mother smiled her approval of this proposal, and then asked, "What will you tell her when you return the nickel?" They finally agreed that the thing to do was for him to go into his classroom early the next morning, and to take the five cents to his teacher saying, "I'm sorry I took what did not belong to me; and I won't do it again." Gene and his mother agreed that this apology need not be in front of the other children, but that it had to be given to the teacher by Gene himself.

The next morning Gene was a sober little boy at the breakfast table, pondering how he would face his teacher. His mother, seeing his concern, suggested that she play she was the teacher, so that he could practice his apology with her. He grinned, and together they played out the little drama before he left for school. The final act of the little episode came a week later at the PTA meeting when Gene's teacher told his mother how graciously he had assumed responsibility for the affair, "Like a little gentleman."

*Encouraging balanced spending, giving, and saving* in children is a goal of many parents. They would like to see their youngsters grow up to be neither spendthrifts nor misers. They try to instill an attitude of cheerful giving in their children. This is not always easy, unless it is begun early and guided with loving care through the years. With the child's first allowance, some of the pennies can be set aside for Sunday School; some put in the child's personal bank; and some put aside for his anticipated expenses. When you as parents use the same strategy in allotting your money, and your discussion of the family policies about it, your child finds it easier to follow suit than if you expect of him what you yourselves do not do.

*Large windfalls of cash can be a problem for your child.* Some well-meaning relative sends him more money than he has ever had in his life before, and his excitement is dimmed by his bewilderment as to what he will do with it. This is his responsibility in which you, his parents, can be helpful. You start with getting his ideas on what might be done with the money. You help him weigh carefully each suggestion, by guiding him to see what would happen if he used the money in this way or that. Once he has come to a firm decision you can offer your assistance in carrying out the program you both agree is a good one. He may need help in taking out his first regular bank account. He may ask you to go with him while he selects some special purchase that is beyond his previous experience. The important thing to remember is that it is his money and that he is learning not only how to use it but also much about becoming responsible in its use.

*Should your child work for money?* There are two kinds of jobs for which a child works for cash: in his family and for outsiders. There is a question as to whether a youngster should be paid for his share of the family's regular chores. Should he get money for cleaning his room? For taking his, or her, turn at clearing the table and doing the dishes? For taking out the trash, and helping with the yard work? Many families feel that a son or daughter should have some assigned tasks as part of their responsibility as family members. For these they should not be paid, anymore than you as parents are paid for your work for the family.

Special jobs for which some outsider might have to be hired, however, are negotiable as children's paid employment for the family. When one of our daughters wanted extra riding lessons (during her horse era), she contracted with us for washing and waxing the car, cleaning the windows of the house on the outside, and other such jobs at rates comparable to what we might have paid outsiders. She was expected to do good work, which was inspected before payment was made. This contract basis of employment worked out well during the time that she wanted extra cash for special projects. It is a scheme that might work in other households, as well. Its advantages are several: the child does not have to beg for handouts; he, or she, assumes responsibility for financing special interests himself, and the youngster is expected to carry out the terms of the contract with the family in responsible ways for which payment is made at rates that are negotiated between child and parents.

*When your child works for others,* you may have to make sure of his safety before approving his taking the job. Baby-sitting jobs for families in the neighborhood are usually all right; but care should be taken to be sure that the hours, the responsibilities expected, and the conditions in the family are such that the sitter as well as the little ones being cared for are protected. Training courses for prospective baby-sitters offered by schools and community agencies help prepare a young person for his responsibilities on the job.

Many a boy, and girl, have their first paying jobs carrying newspapers, or working for a nearby business establishment (as stock boy, bagging girl, etc.). Such jobs are usually protected by standards for employing minors but even then should be a legitimate concern of the youngsters' parents. Questions of how many hours work in a given period of time a youngster can afford and still do justice to his studies and time for wholesome play are matters of responsibility for parents as well as the child himself.

## Homework and Study Habits

Going to school puts certain responsibilities on both the child and his parents for his ongoing achievement. Studies, both in the United States, and in other countries show clearly that it is family influence more than any other that is significantly related to a child's educational advancement. When you parents back your child's teachers, and encourage his progress in school, your child has advantages lacking children whose families do not take an interest in their schooling.

*Report card signing* is not to be taken lightly. Say what you will about the problems report cards present an anxious child, they do measure his progress in specific subjects over definite periods of time. Your attitude as parents toward your child's report card can be positive or negative. The negative parent is never satisfied with his child's grades; and keeps pressuring the youngster to improve, in often discouraging ways. The positive approach celebrates a child's improvement in a given subject, so that he is motivated to continue to make progress. The celebration need not be elaborate, but it does require family attention and notice. A candle in a cupcake, backed by your smiling recognition of his progress is enough to make your support apparent.

*When a child consistently does poorer work* than he is capable of, your punishment on top of the low grades on his report card may not help much. He probably is no more pleased with his poor report card, than you are. You are most helpful when you take the approach, "What do you think you can do to bring up your grades in this subject?" or "Is there something we can do to help you do better in the next marking period?" Sometimes, a better light over his study area, a definite time for doing homework, or an offer to "hear his lessons" when he wants you to, give the schoolchild the extra boost he or she needs to improve. Your letting him know you care, without being punitive about it, keeps the responsibility in his hands, while giving him the backing he needs at home.

*Fear of failure* increases a child's anxiety. Your son or daughter may get unduly nervous before a school test, cannot sleep at night, and in other ways indicates that he or she is undergoing stress over schoolwork. This is a time for you, as parents, to remind your child that he is expected only to do as well as he can. You are careful not to compare his achievement with any other child's; nor to put him into too heavy competition. His anxiety indicates that he is trying to measure up. Your response as parents is to ease up on your pressure, and to reassure him that he is more important than his marks, and that you love him regardless of his grades. Of course, some stress is all right. Any person mobilizes himself for a demanding stint, in ways that are good, and that give a glow of achievement when the job is well done. It is this healthy "putting out" in an effort to do well that may be encouraged as assuming responsibility for oneself—in school or anywhere else.

## Responsibility in the Community

There are many meaningful volunteer roles that a schoolchild can carry in his community. These benefit his neighborhood. They put him in the mainstream of community life with a sense of purpose and participation. What are some of these jobs a child can be encouraged to do for his neighborhood? They differ from place to place and from time to time. They include such things as: participating in cleanup drives, recycling collections, handbill distribution, UNICEF door-to-door work at Halloween, church and Sunday School projects. Later: work camps, volunteer work with young children, with patients in hospitals, nursing homes, retirement centers, and so forth are included. When you parents do your share of volunteer community work, your children can be expected to do likewise. Sharing oneself with others runs in families as a bright thread of service. It brightens the lives of the less-privileged, it lightens the heart of those who serve and makes for happy, selfless family living.

# 10. DISCIPLINING YOUR CHILD

Discipline is not as easy for parents as it used to be. Children have always presented behavior problems. There never has been a perfect son or daughter. Partly because children have drives that have not been contained. Partly because parents sometimes expect more of them than they can live up to. And, partly because a child must be himself in his own way.

*Parents have few rules to guide them now.* Most fathers and mothers today try to raise their children in a democratic atmosphere. They believe that a child has rights that must be respected. They have been imbued with the idea that a child should grow up in his own way. They remember all too well the firm, often harsh, discipline of their own childhood. They recall their thinking as they were growing up, that if ever they had children of their own, they would raise them differently. So, they have tried to forego the treatment they knew as children, in raising their own sons and daughters. The trouble is that in abandoning the methods under which they were raised, they are left with few effective alternatives to take their place. So, many parents are unsure of themselves, uncertain about what to do to discipline their children. They flounder from one extreme to another with little inner certainty to guide them.

## Being Too Lenient Is As Bad As Too Harsh

*Being too harsh was unnecessarily restrictive and punitive.* It curbed many a child's creative potentials. It limited his development and made him more rigidly conforming than was necessary for his full functioning as a person. It caused all manner of guilts and anxieties that made for a child's poor adjustment. If often led to his alienation from his severe parents. It could break his spirit, and cripple his sense of self-worth completely. Although some fine persons survived unduly severe discipline in their childhood, they lost much of the zest for life, and their ability to live freely and fully.

In recent decades a wave of permissiveness has given many a parent the feeling that children should be allowed to do as they please. Research and clinical evidence in child development found that each child grows into the unique person he is to become. So, the thought was that a child should be allowed to grow up at his own rate, in his own way. This was interpreted by many parents as meaning that their children should be allowed to be themselves, no matter what.

*Parents were afraid of damaging a child's ego by too much discipline.* Many a mother and father frozen with fear, withdrew from any attempt at controlling their child. They had been told, "Do not suppress your child. Let him express himself, and do things in his own way." Progressive schools were supposed to let children have complete freedom to do as they wished. And, many a parent tried to follow suit. This became a kind of indulgence that was uncomfortable for parent and child alike. It made the parents uneasy, because they were left with nothing to do to curb their youngsters' wildest acting out. It made their children feel ignored, neglected, and uncertain as to where their limits were—if any.

Anyone who has ever owned a dog, knows that an animal is happier when he knows what is expected of him. An obedient dog is a secure pet, who likes to please his family by doing what they have taught him, when he can. Children are much like this. They are not any happier for being allowed complete freedom.

*A child needs limits in order to enjoy his freedom.* He is puzzled by the absence of adult control, and baffled by his own conflicting impulses. He wants to feel that his parents care enough about him to help him manage his instinctual drives that can be so very frightening. One of our daughters one time was overheard telling her friend, with some pride, "My mother won't allow me to do that!" She told us that same evening that Mary Sue's parents couldn't love her very much—they let her take such chances.

*Youngsters sense that love means being cared for.* This is in the double sense of being protected and cared for as a precious person worth safeguarding. Empty sentimentality that says in effect, "I love you so much, I'll let you do anything your little heart desires," can be interpreted as meaning, "I don't care what you do; live your own life and see if I care."

A child (like a person of any age) needs to feel that the special people in his life look out for him. He needs the security of knowing that he will be protected from danger. That some of life's hazards lie in his own tumultuous feelings make him aware of his need for discipline all the more.

*Indulgent parents are not good for their children or for the country.* According to a recent national survey, 29 percent of the Americans responding to the poll felt that permissiveness is the greatest single threat to family life today. Too many parents let their children run wild, to thoughtlessly harm themselves and others. Parents' efforts to be indulgent have showered their children with things, but deprived them of proper guidance. Their children have felt abandoned, neglected, unheard, and unloved, by parents too busy about their own affairs to give their children the guidance they need.

*Permissiveness now is being abandoned* as was authoritarian harshness in an earlier time. Much as parents may yearn for definite rules for bringing up children, they can't go back to the woodshed method of childrearing. Gone are the days when parents believed that they must "break the child's will" and demand instant obedience. Now we all know that a child must learn to do what is expected of him, painfully, step by step, through the years.

Parental indulgence is as bad as too strict discipline. Neither extreme give parents and children the security they both need in their relationships with one another. Both young and old need to know what is expected of them, mutually.

In very recent years most parents are looking for the kind of discipline that will give both them and their children appropriate guidelines. This type of guidance must be realistic in terms of both parents and children. It must be reasonable; and it must work effectively most of the time.

## When to Discipline Decisively

It is hard for a modern parent to know when to put down the parental foot and when to overlook a child's misdeeds. Most parents realize that they cannot keep after their children for everything all the time. They sense that letting them grow up like Topsy with little or no control is quite as bad. But when to discipline, and when to excuse children's behavior is not so easy to determine. So, let us think together about some of the things that your child does that call for firm handling.

*You act decisively when your child is endangering himself or others.* Such misbehavior as the following call for firm handling:

(1) The child is going beyond safe limits and headed for serious harm.

(2) The child is hurting others.

(3) The child is telling lies, beyond the imaginative fantasies of storytelling.

(4) The child is stealing willfully, when he knows what is and is not his.

(5) The child is disobeying deliberately.

(6) The child is "asking for it" in a buildup of objectionable conduct.

Each of these kinds of misconduct is a child's way of testing your control as his caretakers. All of these, and other hazards you could list, hurt the child, and others, now or later. In every instance, your evaluation of the situation is crucial. Sometimes his offense is slight (as in the danger of a climbing child's falling). In other situations, the hazards are great. Your stepping in should be to protect your youngster from life's disasters, but not from its bruises. Your discipline should guide the child toward safe, healthy, good patterns of living.

Your discipline depends on a number of factors; the seriousness of the child's actions, your goals for him, and his stage of development, how you feel at the moment, and your values individually and as a family. Proven principles of effective discipline can be simply outlined, for your guidance. It will take you years to put a fine polish on your parental controls. You as parents must learn, along with your child what works and what does not—for you.

*Children need discipline.* Their wants are often in conflict with their needs. They start out with instinctual drives that must be channelled in order for them to become civilized human beings. Left to themselves, they would eat like animals, dragging their food to a corner and eating it with their fists. Without the controls expected in human society, they would lack the skills of interacting with other persons: language, courtesies, decencies, and kindness—four of a host of qualities that distinguish persons as human beings.

*Discipline is in two stages:* (1) helping a child know what is expected of him without indecisive confusion, and (2) getting the child *to want to* do what is right, as soon as, and as often as he can. It is fairly easy to let your child know what you expect of him as long as your demands are reasonable. If you expect too much too soon, he will be overwhelmed by your demands, and flee from them, or rebel from you.

Getting your child to want to do what is right is best done through love. He loves you and wants to please you. It is as simple as that—and as difficult. Most children try to be like their parents as much as they can. They need to be loved, so they try to do the things that their parents expect so as not to lose their love. When your child loves you, he wants to do what you want him to, most of the time. He strays away from time to time, but he comes back to you when you receive him with loving forgiveness for his misdeeds and give him another chance to follow your precepts.

*Discipline must be clear and firm,* with few exceptions. When your child understands that he is to wash before coming to eat, he should know that this means every time and not just when you are tired or out of sorts. If "once you let me" happens often enough, a child does not know whether you mean it this time or not. Rules should therefore, be clear, firm, and few enough to follow at any given time.

*Discipline lets a child know what he can do* as well as what is forbidden. Good guidance is not just fencing a youngster in with a host of restrictions. It lets him know what is allowed and what is not. A mother tells her school-ager that going to a neighbor's house to play is all right, but leaving the neighborhood is possible only by special permission. She thus makes a clear distinction between what is permitted and what must be negotiated. Putting all the emphasis on what the child cannot do without giving him a vision of the leeway being given him makes him feel unduly restricted. Therefore, a good principle is to accentuate the positive.

*Curb the misconduct, accept the child,* as much as you can. At any age, let the youngster know that you do not like the inacceptable thing he has done but that you still like him without question. Instead of saying, "You are a bad boy," you can phrase it, "What you have just done was naughty. As a good boy, you will learn to act better." The difference is that in telling him that he is bad, he may believe you and get an image of himself as no good. By letting him know that you think he is a good boy who has done something bad, you give him a chance to redeem himself, and try to live up to a good boy image of himself.

In summary, children need discipline: to protect them from danger—inside as well as outside themselves; to safeguard those other persons near them; to become socialized human beings capable of associating with others in healthy ways; to establish a good relationship with their parents as a basis for their security and mutual understanding; and to help them learn how to discipline themselves as soon as they are able.

*Parents need to discipline their children* in order to have their own basic values protected. They need enough control over their children to assure them of a modicum of order in the family. They want to rear children who will be a credit to the family and who can find happiness and satisfaction wherever they are. Parents are the socializing agents in the society whose responsibility it is to see to it that their children grow up as responsible citizens in a free society. This is no easy assignment. But it cannot be avoided. Every mother and father must feel their way toward the methods of discipline that work best for each of their children. Some children require a firm hand, and others respond well with a light touch. It helps to know when to take a no-nonsense approach to a child's misdeeds and when to be more relaxed about what a youngster is doing.

### When You Can Be Lenient

Parents can relax and overlook a great deal of children's normal behavior as soon as they are sure of their own ground. In general, you can afford to be lenient when:

(1) The child is acting his age;
(2) The child does not know any better, yet;
(3) The child is improving his skills and testing his powers;
(4) The child has an accident or makes a mistake;
(5) The child is sorry about the situation;
(6) The child reports his misbehavior candidly.

*Guidance is best geared to your child's developmental readiness.* You have seen in earlier chapters that a child grows through the years in fairly predictable ways. When you understand enough about the normal process of child development, you know what to expect of your child at each age. You become secure in understanding how you best can help your child grow good and strong, at each stage of his development. Your perceptive interest in what your child is trying to do helps you have the patience to live with his immature and often faltering efforts to grow up.

You do not need to do everything at once. You can gear your guidance to your child's critical needs at each period of his life. This helps him best and it keeps you from needlessly worrying about all he is doing that is right for him at his age. Let us look together at what this involves in a quick overview of discipline through the youngster's first two decades.

*Infants need confidence and cuddling.* You can safely relax and enjoy your baby, knowing that your trust of him is basic to his personality development. You do not need to rush into trying to toilet train him, or teach him table manners, or to share his toys. All this comes later when he is ready for such training. Right now your discipline is focused on helping him become a happy, healthy little person, who is just beginning to learn what he may and may not do to please you.

*Toddlers need to touch and handle things.* Your discipline can be based upon assisting your little explorer investigate his world in safety. You do best by providing for his safe investigation with a minimum of restriction. Your guidance is largely planning ahead for his activities so that you, and he, can get on with your work and his. He needs little discipline in eating or eliminating until he himself is ready for using the appropriate utensils. You save yourself a lot of wheel-spinning and him a great deal of frustration if you give him time to learn what is expected with your example and encouragement.

*Babblers try to get through to others in speech.* Your discipline now is positive in talking with him, answering his questions, and encouraging his communication. As he gets into the negative stage that comes between two and three, you can be prepared for his outbursts of anger. You give him frustration outlets such as clay and pounding materials. You do not make an issue of the inevitable temper tantrums that come with his push for independence. You ignore them as much as possible and remove him quietly to a safe place until he is ready to rejoin you. You avoid as much conflict as you can, by postponing the training he resists until he is in the more pliable period that immediately follows.

*Your youngsters are busy learning outside the family circle.* They are discovering other children in the neighborhood. They are finding many things that all youngsters are supposed to do. They are learning that other families differ from yours in some ways. This is the time when your children try out new words and actions they have picked up from other children. Objectionable ones you calmly inform your child not suitable in your home. Beyond that you do not press the point. When you make a scene about the forbidden behavior, you only reinforce it; thereby tempting your child to use it again, and again.

*Schoolchildren are trying to become responsible.* They have much to learn of what school expects of them, and how to manage themselves. You now help most by being backup persons who assist and encourage your child as he attempts to measure up to his new roles and tasks.

Eight-year-old JoAnne came home from school so quietly her mother went looking for her. She found the child stretched out on her bed, looking as though she had lost her last friend. The mother asked: "What is the matter, dear? Don't you feel well?" JoAnne's plaintive response was: "I've been so disagreeable all day, I thought I'd take a rest." The wise mother patted the little girl's shoulder and told her she knew just how she felt. All of us have days like that, the mother assured the child. It's good to recognize that so many of our problems are of our own making. Taking a nap when we're tired often helps. Then talking out our problems can make us feel good again. JoAnne relaxed, kissed her mother, had a good nap, and came out of her blue mood, with her mother's help. By assuming responsibility for her bad day, she had taken a giant step in becoming a responsible person.

*Teenagers and young adults want a grown-up kind of guidance.* They do not want to be treated like children. They need to have a voice in their own affairs. They have to learn one step at a time, for themselves. They get into jams and need their parents to help them get straightened out again. They need parents, and they know it. But the discipline they require is no longer of the "snooper-vision" sort, but of open, kind communication.

One psychiatrist in charge of a program for adolescents says the root of many teenagers' problems lies in parents with the PIP syndrome: Permissive, Inconsistent, and Punitive. Permissiveness is threatening to teenagers who need parental firmness to give them security as they launch out on their own. Inconsistency is insufferable to young people who need order and reliability in their lives. Punitive parents put additional pressures on adolescents already burdened with the many tasks of maturation.

Teenage Gloria gives an example of good parental handling, when she says: "I like the way my parents work things out with me. They don't punish me for getting home late. They give me a chance to explain why I've been delayed. Mother will say, 'Worrying us by staying out so long just isn't like you, Gloria. You are usually so responsible' " This makes Gloria feel all right. She feels that her parents trust her, and she tries to live up to their confidence in her when she can.

*Discipline is in keeping with a child's capacities,* age, development, and temperament. No two children in your family respond the same way to your discipline. You have to fit your guidance to the individual child, as he or she is at the time. The same child requires different handling at one age than at any other. This keeps parents forever on their toes. You learn and grow along with your children, all through the years. Sometimes you do just the right thing, and everyone feels good about it. At others, you make mistakes, and go through the torment of getting things to rights again.

## Your Feelings As You Discipline

Your own feelings about your child, about yourself, and about discipline effect what you do more than any words of mine. When you feel good about your child, you will handle him lovingly and well. When you are happy about yourself, you tend to be relaxed and good for those in your care. When your relationships with the important people in your life are going well, your feelings will be positive, and your discipline will reflect this inner peace. When you are clear in your own mind as to what kind of discipline is appropriate with a given child in any given circumstance, your control will reflect its sureness.

You cannot count on all these factors working favorably all the time. There will be many times when you become so exasperated with your child that you find yourself lashing out at him. You would not be human if you did not take out in your discipline some of your own unresolved problems—in your marriage and in your personal life. If at times you find yourself being harsher than you intended, you can forgive yourself the more readily for knowing that this happens to all parents at one time or another.

*Your impatience with your child* is not a life or death matter. He can handle your occasional lapses from calm kindness if he feels a basic security in his relationship with you. In fact, your "blow-off" may be reassuring to your son or daughter in knowing that you can be pushed just so far. "Watch out, Mother really means it when her face gets red," one boy informed his younger sister. He may be comforted also by realizing that parents are human too and that he is not the only sinner in the family. It is generally agreed that occasional explosions in the family may be helpful in clearing the air. So, don't grovel in self-criticism. Rather acknowledge your own nature and accept yourself as you are.

*Should you admit to your child that you have been unreasonable?* If you can, you are to be congratulated. Acknowledging to your youngster that you have "lost your cool" gives him an example of how to handle his own outbursts of temper. Apologizing openly when you have been unfair to a child, provides your child with the opportunity for forgiveness a youngster needs to develop in his contacts with people. "That's all right, Dad, I do that kind of stuff myself. Don't let it bug you," was the way Ted reassured his father in such a situation. Ted's father had been grossly unfair in trying to settle a dispute without taking the time to get all the facts. When he learned of the injustice he had caused, he openly confessed his mistake to Ted and his brother.

Ted, who had fumed at his father's partiality, now in the face of his father's apology, expressed understanding and forgiveness beyond his years. Had Ted's father stood on his dignity as head of the house, and refused to acknowledge that he had made a mistake a gulf might have developed between him and his sons. As it was, their relationship was greatly strengthened by the father's gracious acceptance of fault and Ted's mature ability to sense what his father was going through.

*Is instant obedience too much to expect?* Yes, it probably is much of the time. In a moment of crisis when fast action is essential (a boat accident, a burning house, or traffic hazard for instance) a parent has the responsibility to expect and get instant obedience. But in day-to-day living, asking a child of any age to snap to attention every time you require something of him is beyond reasonable expectation. Actually this top sergeant approach to child-rearing is not the best in the long run. Discipline that increasingly puts the responsibility in the hands of the child is far better preparation for the future of his development as a person.

## How About Spanking?

Few parents can honestly say that they have never spanked their children. Even fewer children admit that they have ever been subjected to physical punishment. There are many reasons for this: parents do what they had done to them, in a crisis; children often "ask for a spanking" by pushing their parents to explosive exasperation with their continued misbehavior; and almost all parents at times act impulsively by venting their intense feelings through their discipline.

*The trouble with spanking is that it does not work.* Most parents now know that spanking and other forms of physical punishment rarely are effective. Research done on child-rearing practices reports, "The unhappy effects of punishment run like a dismal thread through our findings." Dr. Sears and his collaborators found that parents who severely punished toilet accidents ended up with bed-wetting children. Mothers who severely punished aggressive behavior had more aggressive children than mothers who punished lightly. The simple fact is that physical punishment is not effective in training children of any age. It often is detrimental to the child and to the parent-child relationship as well.

When you do punish, do it in an effort to teach the child something rather than to get revenge. Parents are needed to help their children learn from their mistakes, not to suffer from them. It is your job as a parent to physically protect your child from danger. You would yank your own grandmother back from an approaching truck to save her from injury. You are without qualms as justified in quick decisive action with a child who gets too far out of line for his well-being and yours.

*The time may come when you are punishing more often* or more severely than you sense is right. Then it is wise for you to get help at a local counseling service or with a professional person you trust. It may mean that you have had about all the strain you can take for awhile. It could mean that you need deeper understanding of yourself as a person as well as a parent. Such things happen in the best of families. When they do, parents can take the same attitude they do when some physical illness shows itself—by getting competent professional help before the problem becomes either critical or chronic.

## Keeping Your Perspective

Just because you see yourself as a good man or woman is not enough to guarantee that you will always be good. There probably never has been a parent who was completely satisfied with his own behavior much less his child's. You have to live within your own limitations and strengths in disciplining your children. Sometimes you will do just the right thing in ways that are gratifying. At other times, for reasons that are not always clear, you are less effective. You say and do things that you regret. Sometimes you "are not yourself" and are uneasy about your feelings, your relationships, and your actions. This is the lot of parents honest enough to see themselves as they truly are.

*If you can forgive yourself your mistakes,* you will be easier to live with than if you pretend a perfection you cannot achieve. Christians are fortunate in having central in their faith the doctrine of forgiveness of sins. Christian parents can know that their heavenly Father can comfort, guide, and help them, when they seek him. They can find support in prayer, and comfort in knowing that they too with their children are learning to be good.

# 11. RESPECT FOR AUTHORITY

Is respect for authority too much to expect anymore? When college students call police "filthy pigs" and high schoolers refer to their teachers as "old bags" or worse, what can we expect of our children?

Many parents are concerned about the lack of respect that children of all ages show their elders. You probably are anxious about what is happening to a society in which attitudes of disrespect are considered smart. You may squirm at the insolence of modern youngsters. You ask how to inculcate an attitude of respect for authority in your own children.

### Are Manners Important, Still?

There was a time when many of us saw manners as an evidence of well-brought-up children. Then, parents stressed manners as important in their child-rearing. They knew that others judged their sons and daughters by the common courtesies they observed. They felt few things were worse than an unmannerly child.

In recent years there has been more emphasis upon children "doing their thing" than on manners as such. Mothers and fathers try not to curb their children's enthusiasm. Parents have been imbued with the importance of spontaneity in young people of all ages. Many adults and children today seem to neglect the simple everyday courtesies that used to be a basic part of social life.

*It is not smart to be rude.* This is as true now as it ever was. A modicum of common courtesy is desirable in interaction between persons of any age. Between children and adults, some respect for authority is essential. Otherwise, a spirit of anarchy or of rebellion destroys the sense of order that makes society function smoothly.

You may feel strongly about this. If so, you try to do everything you can to bring up your children not to be "brats." You impress upon them the necessity of showing respect for age, and for persons in positions of authority—teachers, policemen, public officials, adults generally, and parents in particular.

*Should you allow your children to interrupt you?* You may be torn between two desirables in responding to this question. You know how important it is to children to be heard. You want to share their experiences. You sense that when they are bursting to tell you something, they ought not to have to wait until the magic moment has passed. But, interrupting others is rude and inconsiderate. Somehow you must strike a balance between letting your children speak and not allowing them to interrupt adult conversations.

*"I am sorry to interrupt, but . . ."* is an effective way to break into conversations in progress. Sometimes this is a matter of great urgency. You may have heard of the boy who burst into the family circle one day, started to speak, and was told sharply, "Don't interrupt." The lad became agitated, and finally burst forth, "I can't help interrupting, the garage is on fire."

*Parents interrupt their children at times.* Ten-year-old Sara had been on the telephone talking to her girl friend for the past half hour. Mother had to use the phone for an important call. She had two alternatives for handling the situation. She could take the phone from her daughter with a sharp reprimand and an order for its release. Or, she could drop a note in front of the child reading, "Sorry dear, I must use the phone now." The latter approach was quite as effective in releasing the phone. It had the added advantage of demonstrating to the daughter how such a request could be made with courtesy.

## How Parents Teach Respect for Others

Respect is caught as well as taught. When parents respect their children as Sara's mother did, a lesson in consideration was taught. Children learn to respect other people by being respected themselves. This begins at the child's earliest days in the way his mother respects his patterns of eating, sleeping, playing, and functioning. It continues as the child hears members of his family address one another with courtesy. It is instilled as the child himself is treated with consideration.

"Please," "Thank you," and "Excuse me" are magic words

that open doors to others. They should be a day-to-day part of your family's interaction. Just keeping such common courtesies for company diminishes their teaching value. When you request something of your child, saying "Please" helps him learn how to ask others for what he wants in socially acceptable ways. When you ask his pardon for some offense, you are guiding him in the use of "Excuse me, please." You say, "Thank you," to your tiny tot from the moment he first offers you his fist to kiss, his toy to touch, or a smeary bit of food to eat.

*Take the piece nearest you* is a rule that you too can follow when your child offers you a plate of cookies, or a piece of his candy. When you poke around for the most desirable piece, you are showing him it is all right for him to do likewise. This does not mean that as a self-sacrificing parent must take the least desirable piece. You choose the morsel you want from among those nearest you, and show by your behavior your respect for yourself as well as courtesy to the others in the situation.

*Your respect for persons in authority* gets over to your children. When you criticize the preacher's sermon Sunday noon, you undermine your youngster's respect for his leadership. If you side with your child against his teacher when she tries to discipline him, he loses some respect for her thereafter. Harsh criticism of governing officials at any level causes some erosion of confidence in government. This is not to suggest that you refrain from all criticism of persons in authority. It does mean that if you want to instill respect for authority in your children, your own actions must reflect it.

### Should Children Call Their Parents by Their First Names?

Respect for others is shown in the way they are addressed. It is apparent in the spirit of the relationship. It mirrors the family style of its members in their own particular fashion. Some parents like their children to call them by their first names. Others do not allow it. It makes little difference as long as children and adults in the family have a healthy, happy, affectionate respect for one another.

*It's your choice as parents.* You teach your children to call you anything you prefer. It may be Mother and Father. Or Mom and Dad. Or Mater and Pater (as some formal families prefer). Or Ma and Pa (still used in many families). Or Jane and Joe, if that is the way you want it. You set the pattern your children follow. Your danger is in encouraging as cute your little child's use of your familiar names, and then punish him for the same practice when you no longer find it so appealing.

### Respect for Your Children's Friends

Friends are important to a child. All through his life he needs persons of about his own age. He needs to feel that he is a part of his own generation. He wants terribly to know that the other kids find him attractive, desirable, nice to be with. He may try overly hard to please his friends, in an effort to keep "in" with them.

*Conformity to peer pressure* is worrisome to parents. They are afraid of other children's bad influence on their sons and daughters. They feel threatened when they sense that their child confides in some close friend his own age something they as parents wish might have been shared with them.

Research finds that children are influenced by their peers in many ways. The peer culture is especially influential in youthful styles and fashions. Clothing, grooming, hair styles, forms of speech are *in* in one generation, and quite out of style in the next. Therefore, in a sense, a child's friends keep him up-to-date on "what all the other kids are doing." These areas of life are highly visible, but they are not of prime importance.

*Family influence overrides peer pressures* in the basic values and standards of life. These findings of studies over the years can be comforting to parents who are unduly worried about the influence friends have upon their children. They can relax in the knowledge that their sons and daughters follow the crowd in the "skin out" superficials that show, and their parents in the deep inner spirit of the family.

*Respect for a child you don't like* is hard. You see so many things that you disapprove about this youngster your child likes that you are tempted to forbid the friendship to go further. The little friend may lack the breeding you try to instill in your child. He may use inacceptable speech or have unseemly habits. Before you make an issue of the friendship it may be well to find out what your child finds so appealing in it.

*Your child's self-concept* develops out of the way others see him. You respect him and he tends to respect himself. He sees himself through the eyes of his friends, too. When they look to him for leadership, he begins to think of himself as a leader. As his friends look to him for help, he sees himself as one who helps others. When they like him, he feels good about himself. He measures himself against both your standards and the expectations of his friends. Both are important for his development as a person.

You can help by accepting your child's peers. You treat them with courtesy when they come to your home. You avoid criticizing them in front of your child. When some unpleasant feature appears, you privately ask your child how he feels about it rather than forbidding the relationship. Why? Because otherwise you face the danger of driving underground your child's friendships. You avoid the risk of making your child a little snob and curtailing his exploration of how others feel and are in his effort to find himself.

### Respect Your Child's Feelings

It is important to respect the way your child truly feels, in any given situation. You cannot turn off his emotions. They are a fundamental part of him that cannot be denied. You are wise to see them as they actually are: the unpleasant ones (anger, jealousy) as well as the happier ones (joy, love).

*Your child must learn to express his feelings constructively.* He cannot be allowed to go about with his emotions all unbuttoned and uncontrolled. Neither can you dam up his feelings in the hope that they will go away. When you attempt to deny your child's emotions, they either well up into floods or they are driven deep inside to cause him serious damage now or later. Feelings are the driving force of life. As such they must be recognized and respected for the power they have in everyone's life.

*Acknowledge your own feelings* as candidly as you can. When you admit that you feel out of sorts, you help your child know that this is a human condition and not some "spirit of the devil" that possesses him from time to time. Let your child know when you are mad, or glad, or sad. This helps you face your own real feelings. It is a good example to your child of how a grown-up he loves copes with the range of feeling states that each person has. It relieves him of the guilt that comes when he senses your feeling without knowing whether or not it is he who causes your distress.

Your example in respecting feelings is one of your more important functions as a parent. You set the tone of your family in the way you accept and cope with the many feelings each family member has in any given day. As you learn to respect true feelings, and to express them constructively, you give your child a valuable model for his own life.

## Parent-Centered Authority

Authority in your family may rest with you as parents, with the children, or within the family as a whole. Each has its promises and its problems. Let us review each approach.

*Children want their parents to assume authority at times.* Eleven-year-old Maggie rushed in to her mother to ask permission for a hazardous trip. Her mother went into a long series of questions implying her disapproval of the venture. Maggie blurted out, "Just tell me no; I don't have time for explanations."

Many times a child needs his parents to take a firm stand so that he has some reason for refusing unwelcome invitations. If he can say, "My folks won't let me," he is spared being taunted as "chicken" by his bolder playmates.

*The goal of absolute parental authority* used to bend the child to his parents' will. At one time parents expected blind obedience from their children. Parents were autocratic because this was expected of them; or because they had been brought up that way themselves. Some teachers as well as parents still depend upon such absolute control of their children. Their authority is imposed without question. It may work, but it has hazards.

*A child learns that he can rely on powerful parents* to protect him from danger. He learns that it is they and not he who make the decisions in the family. He finds out that his wishes are secondary to his parents' in the decisions that affect him. He grows up looking to his parents for guidance in everything. Alone, he feels unsure of himself, because he has had little experience in assuming responsibility for his actions.

*Parent-centered authority carries over into adult life* either in dependency or in rebellion, or both. A child growing up in a family where decisions are made for him by his parents may become completely dependent upon them. He submits to their will and lets them run his life. You probably know adults in your acquaintance who at forty or fifty or older still are dependent upon their parents. Others rebel from parental control that allows them little responsibility for themselves. They resist their parents' authority as children and leave home as soon as they can. In between are the individuals who alternately submit and rebel. Even as children, they are obedient sometimes and fiercely resistant at others.

*Any society is in danger of dictatorship* when all power resides in its leaders. Subservient people of any age are unaccustomed to assuming responsibility for themselves. So they look to the Hitler-like ruler of their lives. The time comes when they rise up and overthrow him. So, the seeming peace of absolute control tends ultimately to be an illusion. Your family as a society in miniature may be run by you parents. If it is, you run the risks of any dictatorship.

### Child-centered Authority

You know families where the children have assumed control. The parents may be incompetent, or absent, or neglectful. They may believe that children should not be curbed and let them get away with anything.

*Children want to run things* at times. They usually have a wide repertoire of methods for getting their way. They twist their parents around their little fingers. They fight for their rights, over parental protests. Their temper tantrums from early childhood prove too much for some parents to face. Or, their parents may be caught up in an inadequate philosophy of child-rearing that causes them to relinquish their authority.

*Your goal in granting your children complete authority* may be that of letting them learn by doing. You may honestly feel that children grow best when they have most authority for themselves. You may believe in permissiveness as a policy. Your own experience may have been such that you refuse to dominate your children. You may prefer to err on the side of giving them too little control rather than giving them too much.

*Children in child-centered families* learn to rely upon themselves. They do not look so much to their parents as to their own wishes and urges. Because their drives are immature and undisciplined, children can be cruel at times. In a family where children are at the helm there is a tendency to disregard others. Animal spirits take over and chaos results. Golding's *Lord of the Flies* portrays the terror of a society of children without adult controls. Less explosive elements of the same kind of brutality arise at times out of too much child-centered authority within a family.

*Carry-over into adult life of authority* vested entirely in children can be predicted as confusion and lawlessness. When children are undisciplined, they lack the socializing influence of responsible adults. They are no happier for taking over completely. In fact, children whose parents have relinquished their authority are among the most miserable of creatures. Grown to adulthood, these unhappy persons are confused and uncertain. They have few standards to go by. The society they live in suffers from their lawlessness. Anarchy is rarely pleasant for any of its participants, at home or abroad.

### Authority in the Family As a Whole

Authority vested only in the parents may result in a costly peace. Permissiveness in which children assume control leads to anarchy and chaos. The only safe course between these two unpleasant extremes lies in the democratic interaction of all family members.

*Your goal in sharing authority* with your children is that of helping them grow up as responsible persons. Together you face the issues that emerge in your day-to-day living. Your children learn not to be afraid of problems because you are there to help in their solution. You do not take over the decisions completely. Your children get their chance to speak up, and have a part in the jointly developed course you set together. Since the authority resides in the family as a whole, each member participates in it. Each then develops the self-control that keeps him a participating member.

*Children learn to work with others* when authority is vested in the whole family. They are given a chance to think for themselves and to assume as much responsibility as they can at every age as they grow up. They learn how to reach a consensus with others amicably. They discover how to protect their values and to be considerate of those others hold. They learn how to be self-respecting human beings as well as to have respect for others. They have experience in democratic interaction in their families which carries over into adult life.

*Family-centered authority prepares for good citizenship* in a democracy. Its citizens have the ability to guide themselves responsibly because they have learned to do so as children. They have respect for others of both sexes and all ages from their family experience, in free interaction. They cooperate with one another in getting the work done, both in the home and in the larger community. They become contributing members of the larger society as each does what he can and receives what he needs.

Democratic families with power vested in the members as a whole are not as quiet as those in which children are seen and not heard. They are not as free and easy as those where children rule the roost. But for all around good relationships over the years, they have proven to work out best. As parents you find that it takes years to establish a mutually satisfying relationship with your children. You do not achieve smooth decision-making overnight. Consensus building takes time and effort. But, it assures you and your children a good life with one another now and later.

## Reverence for Life

Albert Schweitzer used the term "reverence for life" frequently. He felt, as many present-day Christians do, that life itself is a precious gift. Man, as the steward of life in all its many forms, has the responsibility to protect and nurture living things.

Conservationists today echo Dr. Schweitzer's concern for life itself. They are concerned about the endangered species that are fast disappearing from the face of the earth. They work actively to purify our streams and waterways and to cleanse our air, streets, and countrysides.

*Children and adults work together* to hold back flood waters of swollen streams. They labor side by side in community clean-up campaigns. They join in efforts to learn more about nature in its many wondrous forms. In a Christian home, respect for life in any of its manifestations is inculcated.

Mother and father emphasize with their children the basic brotherhood of man under the fatherhood of God. They bow with their little ones to the ultimate authority of all mortals—our Creator and Master.

# 12. DEALING WITH QUARRELLING AMONG CHILDREN

The squabbling that crops up between children is one of the most exasperating problems parents face. Children's quarrels are often over such trivial things that it is hard to understand how they become so violent. Many a mother wonders what this fighting means. Mothers and fathers ask how to handle their children's quarrels. When a particularly difficult situation has been dealt with, the question arises, "How can we prevent such a hassle from happening again?"

## Are Children's Quarrels Inevitable?

The evidence is that all children fight at some time in their growing years. Some are more aggressive than others and seem bent upon quarrelling at the slightest provocation. Others, docile and sweet-tempered most of the time, become embroiled in struggles with their brothers and sisters upon occasion. Intensive interviews with several hundred mothers by a reliable research team found every mother at some time or other forced to cope with angry outbursts on the part of her children.

*Fighting phrases children use* are familiar to every parent. In almost any family with more than one child, there is heard from time to time the belligerent, "Mine's better than yours." This represents a struggle for supremacy between children. It arises from each child's need to excel. In a competitive society like ours, the race to be first among siblings is bound to occur from time to time.

"He started it," is a frequent phrase of youngsters trying to place the blame for a fight. Parents may unwittingly bring on such a stance by attempting to "get to the bottom of the quarrel" by finding out who began it. This is usually a fruitless endeavor. Oftentimes the children do not know who, or what started the fuss. The first overt act of hostility usually is provoked by some covert act of aggression by another angry child.

*Tattletales are a problem for parents.* A self-righteous child brings a tale of woe to his mother. "Just look at what he did," is the complaint. The mother is torn between rewarding her child for immediate reporting of trouble and discouraging the youngster from becoming a tattletale. One wise mother we knew would ask her child "What did you do to make him so mean?" She did not always get a straight answer, but at least she helped her child see that it takes two to fight and that one child's attack may have been provoked by the other youngster.

## Should Your Child Turn the Other Cheek?

Christian parents are puzzled about whether to teach their children to turn the other cheek and risk being browbeaten by some bully or to fight for their rights as individuals against aggression. Parents find it hard to agree upon the policy they will follow. Fathers often feel it best to teach their sons to fight in order to defend themselves. Mothers are more apt to want their children to avoid open aggression by quietly taking it, or walking away from it.

*Worldwide dimensions of the fight- or flee-question* impress parents with the need to prepare their children for the reality of conflict as best they can. They realize that mankind has not yet resolved the question as to how to handle overt hostility. Men of all nations talk peace, while wars rage around the globe. Billions of dollars go for national defense when the people want freedom to live in peace. Parents are caught upon the horns of the dilemma in trying to bring up their children to live in harmony with one another. What you do depends upon how you feel deep down inside about the whole question of war and peace.

## Why Children Quarrel

It helps to understand the reasons for children's quarrels. There are a number of universal forces that provoke children to fight with one another. Let us discuss a few of these causal factors, and then you may enlarge on the list out of your own experience as parents.

*They are frustrated and angry.* Children are easily frustrated. They are small in stature, strength, skills, and power. They are pushed around by adults who are bigger and stronger than they are. They are challenged by other children in every aspect of their lives. They cannot get their way much of the time. So, they respond to frustration as humans do, by getting mad and lashing out in anger.

*They feel jealous.* Brothers and sisters share the same house, its equipment and facilities. Even more important, they share the same parents whose love they need urgently. So, at times when a child does not feel that he is getting his share of his parents' attention, he becomes jealous of the child he feels is the more favored. Jealousy is not a pleasant state for the child or for his parents. But it is very real, and very urgent, and cannot be denied. When a youngster feels jealous, he lashes out in anger. He accuses his parents of not being fair. He is aggressive toward the threatening sibling in ways that provoke many a fuss between the children.

*They want to be first.* Children compete to be first in line, first in favors, first in any activity where scores are kept. Like their parents and other adults, they like to win. It is hard to lose repeatedly. When a child does not get enough chances to win, he cheats, or quarrels, or refuses to play. None of these responses is encouraged by his parents. So, the child is left with unhappy options unless his parents guide him into situations in which he can succeed at least part of the time.

*They are tired, hungry, or out of sorts.* Quarrels are more frequent when one or more of the children is tired, hungry, or under pressure. One survey conducted by mothers themselves found that their children quarrelled most often in the late afternoon when they were tired from the day's work and play. Just before mealtime, children as well as adults are more edgy and ill at ease. One way of avoiding some of children's quarrels is to maintain a healthful schedule of food and rest in comfortable family routine.

*They release tensions built up at school and play.* A school child builds up a lot of tension in both schoolroom and playground. He rarely is as bright, or as successful, or as favored as some other child in his class. He may be taunted, harassed, and bullied by some disturbed classmate. He and his teacher do not always see eye to eye on classroom behavior. His own conduct gets him into trouble from time to time. When his frustrations pile up, he releases them in the safest place he knows—at home. So, he takes out on his brothers and sisters the tensions he has experienced that day.

## When Children Quarrel

Perceptive parents find out when their children are most apt to quarrel, so as to be able to prevent hassles from developing. You can keep track of your children's quarrels for one week and plot the frequency of their fusses as a basis for your own strategy.

*Between the time they get home from school and their evening meal,* school children tend to quarrel. When they are full of the day's frustrations and low in levels of blood suger, they are prone to scrap with one another. This may be met by an afternoon snack—a glass of juice, a piece of fruit, or whatever is appropriate in your household. When you sit down with your children and hear about their day at school, this snack time has a double value. It gives you a chance to relax with the children. And, it gives the youngsters an opportunity to vent their feelings by telling you what happened and how they felt about the events of the day.

*When injustice has been done,* children quarrel. This is a familiar, "He took the biggest piece," complaint. A simple way around this particular problem is to let one child cut the cake, and the other child choose the first piece. It is not always that simple, of course. Sometimes there is a grossly unfair situation that any normal child should protest. Parents, teachers, and other caretakers find that most children have a well-developed sense of fair play. Adults are wise to be as fair as they can in their distribution of favors and privileges among the children. This does not mean that you must treat all the children just alike. It does call for giving each child his fair share of your attention.

When something unfair happens to your child, he can be helped to see that such things happen to each of us from time to time. It only complicates the problem to make a big issue of it. The child who learns to lose with poise has mastered an important social skill for which he can be congratulated. When he knows how to handle injustices without losing his cool, he has learned an important lesson that will serve him well all his life.

*Children quarrel when things are uneasy at home.* Children get upset when the family undergoes drastic change. Moving may be necessary for your family, but it probably will not be easy for the children for awhile. Then you can expect more fusses, unless you are successful in helping each child feel secure and a part of the activity going on in the family.

Children sense dissension in the family and often respond by quarrelling. When parents argue or complain, the children in the family react in kind by squabbling with one another. A new member of the family can be especially threatening to a child. When the new member is another child who competes for your time and attention, you can expect some evidence of sibling rivalry on the part of the older children.

## Why the Eldest Is So Mean

Your firstborn probably is not as thoughtful of his or her younger siblings as you would like. When you see things from his point of view, you can do a great deal to make it easier for your oldest child to be good to the younger one(s).

*He was once the only child,* and now has been displaced. When he was a baby he had you all to himself. Then along came his younger brother or sister who took all your time and attention as the baby in the family. You help to prepare your eldest child for the new baby by letting him feel that the baby is his as well as yours. But do not expect that this will completely eliminate sibling rivalry. It is not that easy!

*You expect your oldest to be responsible.* You impress upon your firstborn that he or she is now a big boy, a big girl. You make him or her your first lieutenant and place more responsibility upon your firstborn than he or she may find comfortable. So, the oldest child in the family may revert to baby ways when a new baby arrives. He may be rough with the younger children. You must keep him from becoming cruel, of course. But you are wise to let him tell you how he feels and to let him know that you understand. You can help him express his feelings in ways that protect the younger children, at the same time that you make him feel loved and appreciated.

*Younger children in the family usually have more privileges* than were given the oldest when he was their age. Parents generally are more strict in disciplining their firstborn than they are with their later children. Then they relax and allow more leeway than they did with their first. The oldest child may well resent this leniency that he did not have and vent his feelings on his favored siblings. When he complains of your unfairness in giving his younger brothers and sisters privileges he did not have at their age, you can admit that this may be true. But also remind him that he had advantages as your oldest child that no other shares. Let him know that he is special to you. Tell him you understand how he feels. Assure him that he is loved and he will be a happier, more considerate oldest child.

*Younger children are a nuisance.* They get into your oldest child's most cherished possessions. They disturb his collections. They disrupt his projects. They tag along after him and require more patience than many a child can muster. You compound the problem by insisting that he always include his younger siblings in his play. You help by giving him privacy and a chance to protect his treasures from the intrusion of his younger brothers and sisters. You do well to listen to your children's complaints. Not in an effort to argue them out of their feelings. But in an attempt to feel with them as much as you can.

## Reducing Jealousy in Children

Jealousy is the anger that comes from feeling that someone else is better loved. Every child needs to feel that his parents love him. He needs to be loved for himself, and he needs that kind of love every day. It is not enough to have been loved once upon a time when he was a baby, although that was crucially important as a foundation for his later security. He needs to be sure that you love him now, and that you love him enough.

*Do you love all your children equally?* You may want to answer, "Yes, of course." But wait! Does anyone love any two people alike? Actually, you probably love each of your children in quite different ways. This is all right. It is what your children need of you. So, you err when you try to tell your children that you love them all just the same. You know you don't; they sense that you should not. It is far better to let each of your children know without question that you love him for himself.

*Each must be loved in his own special way.* One of your children is a cuddler; another is more circumspect in his expression of affection. Children differ in the way they love and in the ways they like to be loved. As a parent, you learn to respect each child's preferences, and to give and receive affection as he prefers. This is not always easy. If you are a demonstrative person, it may be hard for you to hold back from your more aloof young-ster, and to shower your love on the child who responds as you do. Fortunately most children have two parents, and a number of other relatives, some of whom will click with their types, amounts, and rhythms of expressing affection for one another.

*Recognize each child's special talents.* Every child has certain lovable characteristics that you can applaud. It will not make him egotistical if your praise comes spontaneously and genuinely from time to time. This is one reason why it is a good idea to spend some time alone with each of your children every day that you can. Take one child with you when you shop or go on an errand. Enroute there will be time for a tete-a-tete in which the two of you can achieve a level of intimacy impossible with others in the situation. In these intimate moments, your child can confide his plans. You can talk over his problems. Most importantly, you can point out those potentials and possi-bilities of his that impress you especially. You let him know that you love him for what he is, and for what he is becoming. This is what your child needs from you. It is the heart of the parent-child relationship.

## Curbing Competitiveness in Your Children

Competition cannot be eliminated entirely from a society like ours. It can be minimized by parents who care enough to rear their children without too much pressure to excel. This in itself reduces some of the stress between children in the family, and makes for a more relaxed atmosphere.

*Don't expect your child to be first* all the time. There are some parents who are so eager for their children to succeed that they put undue pressure on them to be first in everything they do. This puts a strain on the children, and on their relationship with one another.

*Making issues about grades is self-defeating.* There are some parents who are never satisfied with their children's report cards. When a youngster has mostly *C*'s and *B*'s his parents ask why he did not get *A*'s. He gets an *A* one month and they expect him to do at least that well ever after. Keeping an interest in a child's progress in school is all right. But putting too much pressure on school children to work for higher and higher grades can be damaging—to the youngster, to his relationship with his peers and with his parents. In time he may rebel and lose interest in school work. Or he may try so hard to measure up to his parents' expectations that he develops a nervous stomach, a facial tic, or some other indication that he is under too much pressure to excel.

*Avoid comparing one child with another.* It is all too easy for a dissatisfied parent to ask a child, "Why can't you do as well as your older sister (or brother) does?" Teachers sometimes compare a younger with an older sibling who got higher grades when in the same class. This accentuates the rivalrous feeling between the children in the family. It rarely motivates the younger child to improve. It only makes him feel that he is not as loved, or as well understood, or as acceptable as the older child with whom he is compared.

*Rivalry arises from wanting to do better than someone else.* Some sibling rivalry is to be expected in any family. When brothers and sisters compete constantly and with intensity, their relationship becomes explosive and quarrels erupt over trivia. This is the "Mine's better than yours!" taunt that so unpleasantly initiates many a children's squabble.

Helpful parents expect only that each of their children will develop his own talents in his own way. They are not impressed overmuch with grades, and comparisons with other children's accomplishments. They are concerned that each of their children has the opportunities he, or she, needs to grow straight and strong and satisfied with his life. This takes some doing, as any parent can testify. But it is worth the struggle. At stake is not only the children's concord now, but their future as persons.

## Reducing Violence

Many a parent suspects that too much violence in what a child sees can encourage him to be aggressive himself. This is being borne out in studies of the effects of violence in television programs, movies, and other media on the aggressiveness of children.

There are some who argue that a child vicariously gets rid of his own hostilities by watching angry people hitting one another on television screens. Actually, studies now find that after watching a particularly brutal scene, children tend to act out what they have seen and to be more aggressive than they had been before.

*Monitoring children's television programs is a good idea.* There are programs with too much sadism, too much aggression, too much rough talk and conduct to be good for children's viewing. Some parents find that their children cannot sleep after seeing a particularly frightening program. They report that their children's quarrels are more hostile after having witnessed overt hostility on TV or movie screen. They feel responsible for regulating their children's viewing intake, much as they supervise what they eat and drink. Parents would not not think of feeding their children garbage. Should they not be quite as careful about what goes into their minds and spirits?

*Accompany the children to the movies sometimes.* One way of reducing aggression in the family is for parents to go with their children to a movie that has not been specifically recommended as suitable for children. This may not be as easy as letting the youngsters go alone. But it has the advantage of letting the parents see for themselves what their children are witnessing. This prepares the parents for questions arising, or for untoward behavior rooting back to one or more scenes in the film.

Parents in some communities are banding together to request managers of theaters catering to children to be selective in their matinee fare. When enough families refuse to let their children attend the trashy, pornographic, or violently aggressive movies, it eventually effects the producers as well as the local theater managers. This is too idealistic? Perhaps, but how else can people clean up the visual and audial pollution that fouls their children's lives?

*Physical punishment sets a bad example.* You may have been brought up according to the "spare the rod and spoil the child" principle. You may regard whippings as "necessary." This no-nonsense philosophy of child-rearing prevailed in earlier centuries, when life itself was hard. A child's survival in a dog-eat-dog wilderness may have depended upon his harsh treatment. It may not have been as necessary as people used to think. It may possibly account for much of the warfare that has gone on in families and between peoples throughout the history of man.

The evidence is that physical punishment teaches children that hurting others is sanctioned by adults. They tend to copy their parents as they attack those who displease them. They even practice venting their anger on their toys. It is not unusual to hear a tiny tot spanking his stuffed animal with the identical tone of voice he has experienced at the hand of an irate parent. Later he treats his brothers and sisters in much the same way he has learned from his parents' discipline.

## Children at Peace with Themselves

Every child needs three things—food and love and room to grow. When he receives these basic ingredients of security, he feels at peace within himself. When he is deprived of one or more of these essentials for healthy growth, he is at war with himself, and with others around him. A hungry, tired, unloved child is a quarrelsome child, "hurting for a fight."

*Quarrelling is kept to minimum* by sensible routines of eating, sleeping, exercising, and growing within an atmosphere of loving care. You parents set the example for your children in getting along with one another. You can try to keep their squabbles within bounds by following these guidelines.

(1) Feed your children before they get too hungry.
(2) Establish healthy rhythms of rest and exercise.
(3) Provide opportunities for each child's achievement at his own pace.
(4) Help your children when they need it, not before.
(5) Set clear limits that your children understand, at every age.
(6) Disapprove violence in any form, anywhere, in ways your children understand.
(7) Do not physically punish your children as a regular practice.
(8) Discourage violence in movies, television programs, and other media.
(9) Let each child know that you love him in his own special way.
(10) Express your affection for one another openly, often, fully.
(11) Keep yourself from getting too uptight or out of sorts.
(12) Let God guide your daily life.

# 13. GROWING UP—EMBARRASSMENT OR BLESSING?

The mystery of maturing in your children comes before you are quite ready for it. It can be met as a normal part of every child's life. It can be welcomed as a blessed boon for boys, girls, and their parents. It can be (and often is) an embarrassment for the several members of the family. How to weather the maturing process in your children is the focus of this chapter. You do not want them to remain children all their lives. But you had not expected them to grow up so fast, and to change so much. Their growing up can throw you off balance if you aren't prepared for it. It is not easy for them either.

## Children Such a Little While!

Growing up comes earlier than it used to when you were young. It is not at all unusual now for children in the fifth and sixth grades to show signs of maturing. By junior high most boys and girls are well on their way to growing up into men and women.

*Kids their own age get their confidences now.* Where once your children came to you with their problems, now you hear them discussing their secrets with their best friends over the phone, or in whispers behind closed doors. This hurts your feelings, unless you are aware of what is going on and what it means to them and to you.

Adolescents typically follow their parents' teaching and example in most of the important inner things. But, as they begin to grow up, they turn to the children of their own age and generation for discussions of clothes, grooming, and "what the other kids are doing." This pulling away from their closest ties to you as parents is a normal part of growing up. You can take it in good grace, as soon as you are not personally threatened by it.

*Understanding differences in patterns of maturing* helps you parents. It helps you help your young adolescents, too. Anticipating some of the ways in which your relationships with your maturing youngsters will change allows you, and them, to make the necessary shifts wisely and well. It is especially important to know how differently various individuals mature.

## Late-Maturing Boys

You have never thought of your son's father as a shorty. But now, you realize that he got his growth into manhood after most of the other fellows his age did. Your son takes after him and his side of the family. That boy of yours is programmed to mature at a slower rate than many of the other boys his age. That is a heartache for him, unless you can guide him into accepting his own pace with a modicum of inner peace.

*Boys not big enough to compete* with the other fellows in their class at school have a special burden in self-doubt. They see other boys no older than they are gain several inches of height in a year and be in demand for basketball, dates, and other prestigious activities. They watch earlier maturing lads gain weight, flex their muscles, and go out for football without standing a chance for more than water boy of the team, at their weight.

*Your heart goes out to your little guy* as you see him struggle with weight lifting and jogging in the hope that he too can build up muscles the other boys his age have. You watch him try to brave through his disappointment when he isn't asked to a favorite girl's party, or is passed over for a sought-after part in the class play. You wish there were some way you could help him, now when he needs you so badly. You can help in very real ways. Here are a few of the approaches you can try.

*Point out that he is built like his father,* or the other men of the family. Remind him that these were all men of high calibre even if they did lack some of the extra inches in their thigh bones. Reassure him that even though some of the other boys are already well into their growth spurt, his time is coming. He too will be able to shave, or grow a real beard, when his built-in timer goes off. He too will get his full growth at the time that is right for him. Right now, he can relax and do some of the things that do not require size and bulk.

*Encourage his special talents,* now. In this respite he is getting from rapid growth, there are lots of things he can do that he can enjoy now and profit from later. If he is musically inclined, an instrument and a place in the band may be just what he needs to get the feeling of confidence he needs. If he's articulate he might go in for public speaking, or debating. If his inclinations go to the artistic side of life, he has time now to build a foundation for enjoying and participating in the creative arts. He may like to write, or study nature, or go in for photography, or any of a dozen different pursuits in which sheer size are not needed.

*Your confidence and pride in him* help him through what otherwise can be a difficult period. Ridicule him as "a little shrimp" and you deeply hurt the later-maturing boy. The girl who brags about her "great big guy" is rubbing salt in his open wounds. You, his parents can ease the way for your son by letting him know how much you admire him. This should not be a sentimental generalization. It can be something you sincerely like about him, that you honestly relay on to him without making your praise too obvious.

### Early-Maturing Girls

The early-maturing girl has just the opposite problem. She begins to look like a young woman when most of her classmates are still little children. She shoots up in height and has to sit in the last row of seats so that she will not cut off some other child's view. Her figure rounds out and she may be embarrassed by looking "bumpy in front." She wants more grown-up clothes instead of the ill-fitting little girl things she's been wearing. She is out of step with her age-mates, and has no place to put her changing feelings about herself.

*Welcoming the young lady in your midst* is of primary importance now. If you are parents who can take pleasure in your daughter's development, some of the positive feelings may get through to her. You can go along with somewhat more grown-up grooming and clothing, without letting her appearance get too far out of line with other girls her age. Most important, you can help her find ways of expressing her more mature feelings, while she is waiting for the little kids her age to catch up with her.

*Early-maturing girls enjoy babies,* and animals, and the caretaking roles of young womanhood. The girl who is big for her age may have especial need now for a pet or horseback riding that includes caring for her animal. The girl-turned-woman may be a particularly good baby-sitter, especially if she is given some training in child development and care. Her nurturing interests may be expressed in volunteering after school to work with young children, or in helping out with disabled children or adults, or even at a nearby nursing home. You avoid the embarrassment of having her maturing interests turn to sex and boys and premature sophistication by helping her channel her newfound feelings into caring for others in personal ways.

## Father-Daughter Temptations

One of the first signs of your daughter's growing up is seen in her changing relationship with her father. Where once she used to cuddle in his lap, now she, and he feel uneasy about such familiarity. Where once she played catch with him, and helped him wax the car, now her interests turn in other directions.

*Showing Daddy she can take care of him* comes naturally to the young pubescent girl. She enjoys cooking and baking and showing her father what a fine wife she will make someone someday. She welcomes the chance to get a whole meal for her father when her mother is away. She dresses up and sits in her mother's seat and pretends for awhile that she is her father's little sweetheart. This is all quite innocent as long as it is taken in stride by her parents.

*Father walks a tight rope with his adolescent daughter.* If he is too loving, he encourages her fantasies of being the special woman in his life. If he is remote, away too much, or otherwise unavailable for her efforts to please him, he deprives her of the healthy chance to prove herself as desirable with the one man she can trust—her father. He is fortunate to have an understanding wife, whom he loves, to keep the father-daughter affection within bounds. No question about it, he normally is his daughter's first sweetheart. As such, he can give her the pleasure of being an attractive woman with confidence in herself as a person.

## Father-Son Threats

By the time a boy is as tall as his father, he begins to look for ways to prove it. He eggs his Dad on to wrestle with him and to compete in various types of activities. He defies his father, partly to assert his own authority and partly to start a struggle between them.

*A father of an adolescent boy is threatened.* As a man old enough to have a son this tall, the father feels middle-aged and tired (as he often is). He can easily resent his son's exuberance and senseless waste of energy. He sees that tall, slim, figure of his boy and sucks in his own tummy. He may adopt a modification of his son's hair style in order to prove himself as young as he ever was. Or, he may criticize his son's appearance with some of the emotional intensity coming from his unconscious envy of the lad.

*Harmonious father-son relationships* emerge most often from jointly held interests. Together the maturing boy and his father build a boat, or put up a lean-to on the back of the house, or erect a weekend shelter. They spend hours repairing the car or working on a surprise in the workshop. In such a setting, the boy can learn a great deal from his father, and vice versa. They admire and like one another as colleagues. They surmount threats inherent in these years by man-to-man talks, and interaction.

*Mother can encourage her adolescent son and husband* to feel good about one another by referring to them as "my men." She may ask which of them wants to fix a faucet or go on an errand. She points out how much the son is becoming like his father and, yet, what special individuals they both are. She is overheard telling her friends what a fine pair they are. She builds them both up, without making either of them feel threatened.

## Mother-Son Ties

The mother-son tie is an especially close one. She enjoys seeing the man emerge from the boy her son has been. She is proud of his broad shoulders, and of his newfound independence. She may become so involved that she may nag him to stand up straight, or to cut his hair, or do something else that will make him even more perfect in her eyes.

*The mother with interests outside her home* gets along best with her son. There is much to be said for the full-time mother. But when her children are maturing, she can become too much in evidence. Her guidance can be interpreted as interference; and her efforts to be helpful as "snoopervision." Her best defense is to pursue some interests outside her home while her children are maturing.

*Father who is away too much makes it rough* on his wife and adolescent son. His wife misses the man of the house, and leans more than she should on her growing boy. The son needs his father now more than ever to guide him, to set limits for him, and to model manhood for him. Sometimes this cannot be helped. Then some other father figure (a grandfather, an uncle, a coach at school, or leader at the YMCA) may play some of the man's role in the growing boy's life.

*Parents in touch with other young people* are more understanding of their own. The husband and wife who lead a young people's group at church or community center know how other kids act and what other young people are doing. They keep in touch with the younger generation, and so are not so disturbed by their own adolescents. Their confidence in youth as well as their sense of being needed by them stand them in good stead in living with their own growing youngsters.

## Mother-Daughter Competition and Cooperation

Mother and daughter both compete and cooperate with one another during the years when the girl is maturing. Their competition is two-way. Mother at times tries to look and feel as young and vivacious as her daughter. The maturing girl attempts to be as grown-up and poised as is her mother. They both want to please the man of the house and may both compete and cooperate in so doing.

*Cooperation between the women of the family* is seen in many ways. They shop together and become engrossed in finding the best buys for the least cost. They make over their clothes and refurbish one or more of the rooms of the house. They prepare meals both for the family and for special occasions when both can enjoy the fruits of their labors. They join forces in religious activities from time to time.

*Mother and daughter help each other.* There is much for which a growing girl needs her mother's help. She may complain about her mother's intrusion at times. But she needs her and she knows it. You, as mother, can profit from your daughter's help upon occasion, also. You learn to listen in order to know what your daughter is thinking, and to feel with her in what she is going through. You turn to your growing girl for her advice on clothing, hair styles, and what is appropriate in specific situations in the community.

## Modesty—Early Sign of Maturing

One of the first signs of growing up on the part of one of your children is a new show of modesty. You bend over to kiss your son goodnight, as you have a thousand times before. But this time, he pulls the neck of your blouse together with an embarrassed grin. You see your pubescent daughter suddenly insist upon a locked bathroom door, after years of leaving it ajar. You hear your budding adolescent of either sex shriek when someone comes in unannounced. You are aware of the secrecy entailed in keeping a diary, or letter writing, or keeping personal treasures.

*Privacy is more than a privilege* to the maturing young person. It is a right, to be respected by other members of the family. Now the young adolescent needs time alone to reflect on his new self that is emerging out of the child he used to be. He must have time to himself to think through the situations in which he finds himself. He yearns for chances to talk out his feelings, over the phone, in notes, and in a diary. He magnifies the importance of these inner thoughts and emotions, since they are so new to him. He feels violated when he discovers someone has intruded into this secret world of his.

Much as you may be tempted, you must refrain from reading your child's mail, listening in on confidential chats, or peeking into the locked diary. Only as your budding adolescent trusts you, can you expect him, or her, to confide some of the concerns that are so perplexing. Holding what is told you in confidence is another important element in respecting your maturing child's need for privacy. When you feel that your mate should know something your son or daughter has told you in private, you have two choices. You can suggest that the child share his secret with his other parent; or you may get the youngster's permission to let his other parent in on the story.

*You two have the right to privacy, also.* You need time together as a pair now when your children are growing up so fast. Studies show that parents of young teenagers have more to say to one another than they have for years.

## Are They Ready for Coming of Age?

How can you protect your youngsters from the shock of physical changes in their pubescence? You want them to mature with the happy positive feelings that growing up can bring. But, with their maturing they are often plunged into situations for which they are not prepared. So, what can you do?

*You parents prepare your children for growing up.* This includes the kind of sex education that has been going on in your home for years, hopefully. Before your children first went to school you had told them about the origins of life. By the time they are midway through grade school, they should know what to expect as boys and girls begin to mature into men and women.

The boy who welcomes the first show of hair on his face, may be embarrassed by his changing voice. For awhile as his larynx enlarges, his voice in speaking and singing is unpredictable. If he is teased about it, it but compounds his distress. When he recognizes his deepening voice as evidence that he is growing up, he, and you, can welcome this natural evidence of approaching manhood.

A boy should be prepared for the seminal emissions that begin soon after his pubic hair first appears. At night while he is sleeping, semen is released from his penis. This usually is accompanied by a sexy dream. The boy may be troubled by the incident unless he has been told that it is a sign that he is becoming a man with a man's feelings and functions. It is nothing a boy brings on himself. It is as natural as sneezing and quite as harmless.

During puberty a girl becomes taller, her hips widen, her breasts develop, and her body rounds out into the pleasant curves of young womanhood. She can be pleased about these obvious signs of growing up if she feels good about herself in other ways. One of the more difficult adjustments a pubescent girl has to make is to her menstrual cycle. It helps her to be prepared for this normal functioning of her maturing body.

*There is no substitute for open communication* between you and your maturing children. You must be able to get through to them with the things they ought to know *before* the new experiences they soon will be having. They should be able to share with you the many questions and worries that arise in many of the situations they face. If you have built up a good two-way system of communication over the years, it will stand you in good stead now when it becomes so urgently needed.

*Other adult confidantes are invaluable.* You are lucky if your youngster has a Sunday School teacher he or she trusts. You can encourage a close relationship between the two of them, to be tapped when needed by your adolescent. Your family physician, a good neighbor, or a particularly understanding teacher may serve as a wise and responsible adult counselor when your youngster needs someone outside the family. You need not fear these contacts. Every maturing boy or girl needs to go beyond the family at times for the sounding board that is needed.

*You cannot protect your child from mistakes.* It is not possible to bring up children without their getting into trouble of one kind or another. Of course they will make mistakes. Hopefully, they will learn from them. If their errors in judgment give them strength for meeting similar problems in the future, you are fortunate. When they learn to face their problems without guilt, they have gone a long way toward meeting life's problems as they arise. As they work through the tangles in which they get themselves, without fear, they gain the confidence they need as young people.

*You help most by standing by* as their first line of defense. You cannot keep this attractive daughter, this handsome boy tied to your apron strings. They are not house plants to be protected from life's chilling winds. They can take whatever comes when they feel secure in your love. They come to you when the going gets rough because they need your strength and guidance. You need not pry, or coddle. Just be yourself, mature, aware, and available. Trust your maturing children, and they will do all they can to be worthy of that trust.

*Growing up is a miracle.* Over the period of just a few years, your little child emerges from childhood as from a cocoon. He towers above his father. She outshines her mother in many ways. You can relax and enjoy this new beauty in your offspring. More than that, you can participate in the miracle yourself, as you see life unfold in your child, in one another, in yourself. Maturing in both generations need not be embarrassing. It is truly a blessing open to all who enjoy growing and becoming.

# 14. PUPPY LOVES AND LITTLE SWEETHEARTS

Your child has loved others before. By the time a boy or girl gets into the teen years he or she has become an old hand at loving. When he could barely lisp her name, your son discovered a special affinity for his little girl cousin. You found them sitting close together on a rock, arms around one another that summer at the cottage. He looked up with a heaven-sent expression on his face announcing, "We're tousins!"

Your daughter had a crush on your next door neighbor when she was barely three. You used to have all you could do to keep her from following him around like a faithful puppy. When your son went to kindergarten, he fell in love with his teacher. His first-grade teacher could do no wrong, in his eyes. Throughout the years of children's growing up they love a wide variety of others of both sexes and of various ages.

## You Feel New Threats Now—Why?

Now when your young teenager floats into the room with that "I'm in love, I'm in love, I'm in love" look in shining eyes, your heart skips a beat. You feel real fear at what having a sweetheart now could do, to your child, and to you. Why should you feel so panicky? What are you afraid of now that did not threaten you before?

*You are afraid that your adolescent will get carried away,* and do something foolish. You recognize that being in love at fourteen or fifteen is not quite so harmless as it was at four or five. Now these early-maturing kids of yours are physically ready for sexual expression, long before they have the maturity to handle their feelings. It will be years before your youngster is ready to marry and settle down. There is a lot of growing up still to do before he has found himself and is ready to choose a life mate. Preparing for one's life work is important for both a boy and a girl these days. That calls for educational and vocational experience. You do not want your young teenager to sacrifice a promising future by getting in too deep too soon.

*Teenagers today are especially vulnerable.* They face hazards that were relatively rare in an earlier generation. Now drugs taken innocently or on a dare at a party can make them do "crazy things" you fear. Drinking among high school students in your town frightens you. Alcohol is bad enough in itself. Combined with dating and driving, it can become an explosive combination. Almost any evening you bid your youngster good-bye with a "Have fun, dear," while in the back of your mind you think, "And, do be careful!"

*You fear you have not prepared them* for everything they will face. You probably have warned them about the dangers of venereal infection. Hopefully both the boy and the girl know enough about conception to avoid the dangers of unwanted pregnancy. But have they control enough to put their knowledge to work when they need it? Are they ready to cope with the exploitive person who is too much for your teenager to handle?

### What Does He See in Her?

You parents are rightly puzzled about some of your son's choices in girls. You soon discover, however, that quizzing an adolescent in love is far from satisfactory—for him or for you. So, you bite your tongue and try to have faith that your boy will come to his senses.

*Mother sees the girl from a different point of view* than does her son. She notes her lack of good manners, her casual possessiveness, and her bold assertiveness. Her son sees the sureness with which she handles the many areas in which he still feels uncertain. Mother observes the girl's full-blown figure. Her son rates high with the other fellows for having "such a dish" for a date. Mother senses the girl's reluctance to be friendly with her. That may be what appeals to the boy who is trying to emerge from his too-close dependence upon his mother. Mother wonders how her son could be attracted to such a mousey little thing; while her son loves the feeling of being the strong, sure one in his affair with his little sweetheart. You may not know the reason for your son's choice of girls. He may not be able to tell you. But you can rest assured that there is a real reason why he has fallen for this particular girl at this time.

*Being courteous to your son's sweetheart* is a must for you as parents. If you criticize her openly, you only widen the gulf between you and your son. If you treat her coldly, you turn her off, also, and risk her hostility in return. It may not be easy, It usually isn't. But you must do what you can to accept your son's sweetheart with courtesy.

*Chances are he will end up with someone like his mother.* Typically a teenage boy goes through a series of little love affairs before he finds the woman with whom he wants to spend the rest of his life. That final choice more often than not is a young woman very much like his own mother in many respects.

So, you as parents can afford to relax. You can take the girls your son takes to without fear. You may never know what he sees in any one of them. But you can be sure that if your family has been a fairly happy one, in time your boy will want to make his own home like that if he can.

### How Can She Love That Gangly Adolescent?

Comes the time when your lovely adolescent daughter dashes to the phone whenever it rings. It might be *him* you understand. She moons over a note he passed her in school and waxes ecstatic about him when she's in the mood. At last he comes around, and you see this Adonis for yourself—pimply faced, arms hanging loose, feet falling over the furniture, the epitome of clumsy adolescent boyhood. What can she see in him? Mother smiles indulgently, as though she knows. Father is shocked at what poor taste *his* daughter has, when she has been provided with such a model of manhood at home.

*Could father's nose be out of joint?* Why not? This daughter of his has been his little sweetheart for years. He has told her so. She has put on all her charms for him; still does in fact. It hardly seems possible that with such affection between the two of them in the family, she could possibly fall for such a callow youth. Her father broods about her boyfriend and what may be happening as soon as they leave the house. It is all he can do to keep from teasing her about the affair. He tries to keep the scoffing out of his voice when he speaks to the lad, because he realizes that ridicule will only throw the young couple closer together than ever.

Rest easy, Father. Your daughter is just putting her toes in the pool of available boys these days. By the time she is ready to slip completely into the sea of matrimony, she will have known many kinds of boys, in many ways. Eventually, if she has been as happy with you as you would like to believe, she will end up with the closest reasonable facsimile of the kind of man you are. You can afford to wait. In the meantime, relax and watch from the sidelines.

*Maybe she can cope with this boy.* More sophisticated fellows may be too much for her just now. Older, smoother customers take a great deal of social skill on the part of the girl. Your daughter now is but beginning to find out what she can handle in boy-girl relationships. If she starts with "Gentle Joe," it may be because she needs gentleness more than anything else in her sweetheart right now.

### Crushes on Older Persons

The one-sided love that a young teenager showers upon some special adult is puzzling to many a parent. You wonder why he does not fall for someone more nearly his own age. You worry lest the adult your youngster has chosen can be trusted with such special affection. You do not want to see your adolescent hurt before he or she gets a chance to mature completely. It would be awful to have such a precious gift of love exploited. Besides, why some other adult instead of you parents who have always been so close?

*A boy's attachment to his coach is natural.* Most boys go through a stage when they will do practically anything the special man in their lives suggests, out of sheer adoration. This lad of yours rushes out in the morning to get the equipment out for the coach. He comes home late in the afternoon, because he's had a chance for a special workout with his beloved coach. Father may be out of patience. Mother may be worried about what is going on. Both should know that a lad of your son's age must explore other adult styles of life. He has to try on for size especially meaningful relationships with a number of other persons as he grows up. Usually he chooses some fine man (a coach, a teacher, guidance counselor, or neighbor) to lavish these special attentions on. As long as the man does not depend upon the boy's affection to meet his own emotional needs, he and the lad and you will come through all right.

*When your son moons over an older woman,* you need not panic. If your memory goes back far enough, Father, you'll remember such a love in your own adolescence. It may have been your best friend's older sister who was the love of your life for awhile. You slipped her little poems from time to time. She filled your dreams night and day. If she was nice to you, you could wilt with joy. If she scorned you, you went through torture. It did not last very long. But it was very real and bittersweet for awhile. So it is with your son's first crush upon some older woman in his life. You need not make fun of it. In fact, you need not do anything about it. It's part of growing up, emotionally. When your boy no longer has need for it, it will be over as fast as it began.

*Is your daughter too fond of a favorite teacher?* If she is not now, she possibly will be in time. Most adolescent girls go through a period of strong emotional attachment to some woman outside the family. It may be a teacher, a nurse, a celebrity your daughter has never met, or almost any adult female whom she suddenly finds overwhelmingly lovable.

*Love for a married man* need not be illicit. Your adolescent daughter goes out of her way to spend all the time she can at church. You finally discover that it is not only religion but the pastor whose magnetism draws her there so much. She praises him every chance she gets. She talks about him constantly. He is a good man, and you can be pleased that she has chosen someone so admirable as the object of her affection. By now your preacher has learned how to deal with adolescent girls' crushes so that they do not get hurt. He knows from experience that such intense admiration is soon over, but that it is very real while it lasts. If you have any question, he may be able to reassure you about it in a personal conference.

More difficult to deal with is the crush your daughter may have upon the father of the children she occasionally sits with in the evening. He drives her home after her time at his house is over. This means that the two of them are alone together for a few minutes in the car. At her age, she may misinterpret his gallantry in opening the car door, putting his hand under her elbow as she gets out, or in any of a hundred different ways that the boys her own age have yet to learn. Unless he exploits the situation, the relationship can be quite innocent.

## Buddies of the Same Sex

During the early teen years, your child quite probably has

a best friend with whom everything is shared. They are chums who everyone who knows them sees as having an especially close relationship. One is rarely seen without the other. They obviously mean a great deal to one another. As parents, you may wonder if they are perhaps too close? Should not your child divide his affection with others? Are there inherent dangers in same-sex friendships?

Two girls of about the same age have much the same experience in life. Best friends of the same sex are to be expected early in adolescence. Two boys confide their deepest thoughts with one another. They share many of the same uncertainties. Their interests and activities are similar. They dream the same dreams, look forward to the same future. Together they share a common culture, and make one another feel secure. In time they may pull apart, or they may remain good friends for many years. Whatever the outcome, chums of the same sex are a normal part of growing up for members of both sexes.

*True homosexuality does not suddenly make its appearance* in the early teens. It roots back to early relationships in childhood, according to specialists who have studied the problem. There is a same-sex tie that can be very strong during early adolescence. But this is soon outgrown for other forms of love, if the youngsters have had a fairly normal childhood.

Modern-day thinking makes much of homosexuality. This scares many parents more than it should. If your child has homosexual tendencies it is not because of the best friend he or she has now. Such buddy-buddy relationships are a normal part of growing up. At most they are temporary; at worst they continue beyond the point when other loves should be making their appearance.

*Including the best friend in family plans* is generally a good idea. The two adolescents will enjoy the occasion more together than they would if they are separated. Your son or daughter may go reluctantly with you on a family jaunt. But if his or her friend can come along, the whole experience is more enjoyable.

The rest of the family is free to enjoy themselves when the adolescents are happily involved with one another. This is a time when the young teenager needs someone besides family to enjoy. He or she is growing up to the place where family alone is just not enough. When you include the teenager's best friend in your family plans, you give the whole family a chance to have a good time, as well as provide for your adolescent's emotional needs.

## Does Puppy Love Last?

We know couples who have loved one another all their lives. They were childhood sweethearts. They loved only each other all through high school and college. They remain devoted lovers after years of happy marriage. This does happen, but it is not usual.

*Puppy love rarely lasts but a few months.* Most young people experience a series of infatuations that their parents see as puppy love. It worries many a mother and father to see their son or daughter so intensely involved with a little sweetheart. They worry lest the young couple's feelings sweep them off their feet. They know that in all likelihood this affair will last no longer than earlier ones have. Then comes the break-up of the couple and the possible hurt of their own adolescent.

*Taking a little sweetheart lightly is ill-advised.* Regardless of how temporary you parents may feel the current love may be, it warrants your respect. Your son or daughter is caught up in the beloved at the moment. Having one's feelings questioned or being ridiculed for having them is no help. Rather your son, or your daughter, needs your quiet support now while feelings run high. You can respect the emotions involved even if it is difficult to hail this young love as the great love of all time.

*Living through young love* requires patience. Your steady standing by is needed now when your youngster is in the turmoil of love feelings. You have to take the babbling on and on about the beloved's charms. Even more difficult is to accept the moodiness that comes to any adolescent in love. The closed door, the secret phone calls, the intensity with which invasion of privacy is attacked, all have to be taken in stride. In time, this too will pass, and your young teenager will return to the family, for awhile.

## Broken Hearts Do Heal

When a puppy love affair ends, there is apt to be a broken heart in your family. Some teenagers report a feeling of relief when young love breaks up. But most put on a show of misery, especially at home. With their peers they may stage a big act of how grand it is to be free again. It is you folks at home that get the brunt of the anguish the youngster feels.

*Breaking hearts do heal in time.* Your adolescent may not be sure of this. He, or she, feels so miserable that nothing seems possible now. The future looks black. The present is impossible. The past has all been a big mistake. As parents, your experience in early loves gives you a broader perspective. Your calmness now can be encouraging. If you are available, with respect for what your youngster is going through, your attitude itself is encouraging.

*Listening with compassion eases a broken heart.* You have to fight the urge to pry. You may be curious as to just what happened to break up the young lovers. But your best course is to refrain from questioning. If you are available with a listening ear when your adolescent is ready to talk about it, that will help. Then your perspective and counsel may be comforting, if you are careful not to overdo it.

## What Adolescents Learn from Their Sweethearts

Painful as young love may be at times, it is good experience. There is nothing like having been in love to know what others go through in their time. Literature, drama, art, music now seem relevant, because the young person has felt the emotions that are being expressed.

*Understanding and gauging their own feelings* is learned through experience. In time, your youngster learns that emotions can be strong without being lasting. He becomes wise in recognizing the many ways in which a boy can be attracted to a girl. She discovers how differently she loves the boys in her life. By young adulthood, hopefully, your youngster will have had enough experience in loving to be able to tell how significant a particular love feeling is.

*Learning why limits are needed is important.* Members of both sexes must discover for themselves the pull of physical attraction, and how to control it. They must respect the limits adults set for them, at home, in school, church, and in community situations. This comes from wise adult counsel when they first meet the problem.

*Developing a repertoire of interaction in love and out.* During the teen years a boy or a girl is gaining the social skills that will be needed all the years ahead. The fellow is slowly gaining the social poise he needs with girls. The girl is becoming adept at accepting the attention of the boys she likes and brushing off others without being rude. They all are discovering the many, many ways in which they can express their feelings for one another. They find out that some of the deepest emotions do not demand immediate gratification. They learn that the sexy girl or boy may have very superficial interest; while "good old Joe" may feel very deeply for his beloved.

With one boy a girl feels deep down good, with another she senses a feeling of naughtiness in their contact. With one girl a boy feels mature beyond his years, while another makes him feel like a little kid. Some loves are gay and lighthearted, others are so serious both of the pair are depressed after being together. Parents can help their young people sort out these tangled feelings, so that a full complement of emotional expression becomes familiar in time.

### Being Available as Parents

Your teenagers may make you feel that you should "get lost" when their friends are there. But, your place is there. You do not need to be underfoot. You need not be obvious about your availability. But when your teenager has friends in, you belong somewhere nearby.

*Being there is important.* It is not that you do not trust your teenagers. It is more that you represent the adult guidance that is often needed when teenagers gather. Liza could not handle the uninvited guests that came to her party and began rough-housing. Two of the older boys had been drinking and would not listen to reason. She was relieved to have her father step in and send the rowdy fellows on their way.

*Setting reasonable limits is your responsibility.* Teenagers need parents to establish the boundaries beyond which they are not to go. When Archie's mother discovered that couples were going upstairs and turning out lights in the bedrooms, she calmly but firmly turned the lights on and sent the couples back downstairs.

Suitable conduct, hours for getting home, appropriate grooming and clothing, acceptable language, and attitudes of mutual respect are all matters for parents to enforce for and with their teenagers. Many a well-meaning young person is swept along with the crowd unless some responsible adult firmly and with good humor sets the limits most young people need.

# 15. GETTING THROUGH TO TEENAGERS

There are many ways in which today's teenagers make it difficult for their parents to get through to them. The problem differs from family to family, and from one youngster to another, but there are certain universals that plague most parents today. Among them is the perpetual noise with which teenagers surround themselves.

### How Hard It Is to Communicate

*Loud music makes conversation impossible.* Modern music seems to demand of young people the highest possible setting on the sound button. It is practically impossible to hear one another without shouting above the tumult. A thoughtful parent hesitates to yell, "Shut that thing off, so I can talk to you." That approach could hardly be expected to bring about the atmosphere for a cozy chat. So the adults of the family suffer in anything but silence while their teenagers block them out with their own special sound barrier.

*Closed doors marked "Private"* are hard for many a parent to take. One father tells of coming home tired one evening to find such a sign on his son's door. The father removed it without a word. The next day it was replaced by a second sign that read, "Do not disturb." That too was taken down by the boy's parents. By the third day an even larger sign "Keep out, this means you" appeared on the door to the lad's room. By then the parents felt that something had to be said beyond sign language. In questioning the boy about why they were so obviously being shut out of their son's room, his reply was, "All I want is a little privacy." They let it go at that, but it was not easy for them.

*Feeling turned off is hard.* Parents have often told me me that their teenagers seem to turn them off as they would the "off" button on the radio. When I ask if there are any particular times when they realize that their youngsters just are not listening anymore, it takes them a thoughtful interval to report that it usually is when they are "trying to tell the kid something for his own good." Using the analogy of the off button, I sometimes ask the parents at what point they turn off a program to which they have been listening. Someone is sure to suggest that it is when they have heard the program before or are getting a particularly unpleasant commercial. All that is needed to drive the point home is to smile! Teenagers turn parents off when they've heard it all before or when what the parents are saying is especially unpleasant just then.

*Listening to teenagers' nonsense* can be unpleasant to adults. While some fathers and mothers enjoy their youngsters' silly talk, others find it boring or downright disagreeable, especially when they are trying to talk sense to the young persons. One perceptive mother sees that her adolescents begin to kid her with their double talk at the very times they have had enough of her "sermonizing."

## Teenagers Talk Freely with Each Other

When this topic was announced at the beginning of a parents' meeting, one father's whispered comment could be heard above all others, *"Freely?* You should see my phone bills!" This Dad was all too aware of how easily conversation flows between his teenagers and friends their own age. He and his wife had had to insist upon the use of an egg-timer at the telephone table to limit the length of their teenagers' telephoning. Other families establish rules about no phone calls at meal time or during those intervals when father is expecting an important business call. In desperation, some parents have given their teenagers their own phone, so that the rest of the family could use the family phone in peace.

*Similar experiences are shared by young people* of the same age. They know the same teachers, go to the same school, and run around with the same group of other teenagers. Their days are marked with similar successes and disappointments. Their conversation is marked by attempts to evaluate experiences they have shared, and to unravel problems they have met together. It is no accident that two girls talk on and on over the phone when they have said good-bye to one another not half an hour before, after school or a social occasion.

*Styles are set by the young generation.* It is the younger set that determines what clothes are appropriate for various occasions. "What all the other kids are wearing" becomes terribly important for a young teenager eager to look like everyone else. In this sense, friends his own age are a better source of information than are parents, who had their time conforming to rigid adolescent styles a generation ago.

If the length of your son's hair bothers you, it probably can be chalked up to what the other fellows his age and a bit older tell him is right. You are wise not to make too much of an issue about it. There are other concerns of more permanent value that should not be sacrificed for what can be changed by a whim, a shift in mood, and fifteen minutes in a barber's chair.

*The generation gap widens over the years.* Studies find that adolescents' orientation shifts from parents to peers over the years they are growing up. Nine out of ten fourth graders follow their parents' lead. By the sixth grade the percentage has dropped to eight out of ten, by the eighth grade four out of ten, and less than one third of the tenth graders look to their parents before friends their own age. In the meantime, percentages of boys and girls turning toward their peers steadily increase from less than 6 percent in fourth grade to 40 percent in eighth grade, to nearly half by the tenth grade. Especially is this true in such superficial things as appearance, styles in speech, music, recreation, and humor. Parents continue to hold the inside track as basic character molders.

You probably are closer to people your own age right now than you are to your mother and father. The simple truth is that each generation must find itself within its own time. In a fast-moving society, this makes for some generation gap, especially during the teen years.

## How Adolescents Feel About Their Parents

During the first two decades of an individual's life, he grows toward complete maturity. In his maturing, he moves from the complete dependence of infancy, through to the independence of adolescence and hopefully on to the final state of interdependence characteristic of adults. Let us look briefly at each of these stages of parent-child relationship, for the perspective they give on the full sweep of maturation.

*The dependency of infancy lasts but a little while.* During that time the baby is completely dependent upon his parents for everything he needs. His very helplessness is appealing; and caring for him satisfies the nurturing impulses of mothers and fathers. But his dependency is soon eroded by the baby's eagerness to do things for himself. As soon as he can, the healthy young one backs away from his mother and asserts his budding independence. This stretching away from childish dependence goes on all through childhood until it climaxes at adolescence.

*Fighting for independence is characteristic of adolescence.* It is during the teen years that a youngster has to develop a sense of his own autonomy. This means pulling away from his parents far enough to feel that he is his own person. He needs to develop competence in making his own decisions. He must learn from his mistakes, as well as his successes. This is not easy for him, or for his parents. He struggles to be independent, as of course they want him to be. But his insistence upon being let alone is difficult for parents.

Teenagers' fight for independence is not only against their parents' interference, but against their own immaturities, not quite outgrown. Someone has observed that an adolescent takes one step backward for each two steps forward toward maturity. He pushes ahead boldly toward the independence he must have, and then in confusion rushes back toward the safe haven of his parents' security when he is hurt. His most violent conflicts are usually not over anything his parents have done, but rather out of his own uneasiness about himself. Parents, aware of this self-questioning, so common among adolescents, can do a great deal to build up their teenagers' self-confidence with their support and reassurance.

*Becoming interdependent persons takes a while.* Mature adults know that they can no longer be dependent as babies. Nor is it possible for any one individual to be completely independent of others. All men are related to one another. Each needs others for survival, for enrichment, for companionship, and the meaning of life itself.

The time comes, usually late in the teen years, when a young person gets over his insistence upon independence, and begins to relate in more mature ways with his parents. This opens up a whole new relationship that has many rewards for members of both generations. Now they can work together without threat of domination and submission. Now they can talk man to man, woman to woman. Grandmother can tell you of the joy it was when her daughter grew up enough to enjoy as a young woman, sure of herself, and willing to be openly free and fond of her mother as a person.

*Open criticism is a mark of autonomy.* Young teenagers tend to be critical of the things with which they are surrounded. They fuss about the furnishings of the home. They complain about the vintage of the family car. They are embarrassed to have their friends see things the rest of the family find quite acceptable.

By the middle teens, young people become more openly critical of the members of their families. A sixteen-year-old girl insists that her mother get a new hair style, or that she buy some new clothes. She criticizes the way younger children in the family are being disciplined. In many ways she suggests, not too kindly, that she could do a much better job than her mother is doing. This may be whistling in the dark. It can be hard on the mother's ego and rough on the mother-daughter relationship. But it is one way that a girl convinces herself that she too is becoming ready for a woman's roles. Similarly the teenage boy criticizes his father as one way of asserting his own autonomy as in a man-in-the-making.

Understanding the reasons for teenagers' critical attitude in the family helps many a parent find the patience needed to weather what otherwise might be a stormy period. When you can view your teenager's unpleasantness as evidence of the budding maturity taking place, you can find the support both you and your adolescents need.

*Teenagers admire their parents* more than they admit. Studies find that teenagers generally admire their parents more than they do themselves. They tend to think more highly of adults than do the adults themselves. Much as they openly criticize the grown-ups in their lives, young people secretly realize their superior wisdom and experience. At a time when young people are trying to become mature men and women, they are drawn toward the adults in their lives and try to become like them if they can.

You do not have to insist upon your teenagers' respect or admiration. You have it more than your older children openly acknowledge. When they become hard to live with, it probably is because of their self-doubts rather than their rejection of you.

## Why Parents Lose Their Patience with Teenagers

You are an exceptional parent if you never lose your patience with your adolescent children. There is much in your relationship that annoys and upsets you. Recognizing some of the reasons for your emotional upheaval where your teenagers are concerned may help you deal with it.

*Parents are understandably afraid for their teenagers* today. It has never been easy to grow up. Nowadays, there are so many hazards in the lives of the younger generation, you parents naturally are concerned. You worry about them when they have the car out, for fear they will drive too fast or park too long. You are anxious about teenagers' use of drugs, alcohol, and tobacco that has become so much a part of the current scene. You would like to protect them from irresponsible sexual activity. You may trust your own teenagers but wonder if they can handle the pressures they face from others their age and older.

You have two strong forces working for you. Your adolescents can be expected to follow their early home training in most respects, and they will come to you for guidance if you keep communication channels open in the family.

*You are afraid of your teenagers* at times. They seem so big and brash and sure of themselves, your opinions wilt in open confrontation. Many teenagers are bigger than their parents and grandparents both in stature and weight. They are growing up earlier, and becoming bigger than earlier generations in the same family. They are coming of age at a time in history when the little people of the world have been insisting upon a hearing. So, they sound off loud and strong with an absence of deference that used to be shown elders by young people.

*Does your influence continue?* Now, when your young people are making the most important decisions of their lives (education, life work, religion, friends, love, sex, and marriage choices) you wonder how potent your influence is. Will the values you have tried to inculcate carry through effectively? Can you rest assured that the early training you gave your children will be strong enough now to protect them from life's temptations? Is your love and theirs for you great enough to steady them in stormy times?

You can be relatively sure that if your relationship has been a good one, your children will not depart too far from the way of life you have shown them to be good. At the same time, you must face the fact that every young man and each young woman must find his and her own life style.

Mistakes will be made in the fumbling trial and error of attaining selfhood. But, life teaches through failures as well as successes. Your best approach to the foolish things your young people do, is to calmly help them appraise the nature of the problem and to solve it with all the resources they have.

### Teenagers Need Parents—and They Know It

Your adolescent may come to you for guidance on the big issues of life. He wants to talk over his career plans from time to time. Do not be fooled by the offhand way in which he raises questions about what he might become. When the query arises, he is looking for your response in as clear and calm a way as you can muster.

*Most teenagers want their parents' help* with problems of proper conduct in the various complicated situations they encounter.

*They look for limits within which it is safe.* Teenagers need parents who set reliable limits within which it is safe to be free. The youngster with indifferent or unsure parents is left to founder.

*Adult models—where are you?* All through the teen years, young people seek worthy adults to emulate. They start with their parents' example. When this is satisfying, they tend to hold to it while exploring other ways of being a man or a woman. It is then that they turn to a favorite teacher, coach, or other admired adult as "model of the month" as one mother terms it. During that time, the adored older person is often quoted at home, his or her appearance and speech is copied, and tried on for size. Then, some other hero or heroine holds the youth's attention for awhile. By identifying with various adults, your adolescents explore ways of life that might be possibilities for them.

### Parents As Confidantes

Your maturing sons and daughters continue to come to you with their confidences as long as you do not abuse their trust. There are a number of ways that parents turn off their adolescents without meaning to do so. Let us review the more common mistakes parents make in their efforts to be helpful. By being aware of the usual barriers to continuing communication, you may be able to avoid them.

*Nagging and lecturing cuts confidences.* Paul would like to go to his father more often for man-to-man talks. But he finds that whenever he raises a personal topic for discussion with his dad, the older man launches into a harangue full of criticism and warning, rather than of attempts to be helpful. Paul feels as though his father criticizes everything he does. He says he cannot do anything that pleases his parents. They nag and scold and remind him of his faults, until now he avoids them as much as possible. It is possible that Paul's parents do not realize how critical they are of their boy. They are trying so hard to "make a man of him" that they have let themselves become unduly critical of whatever he does, and attempts to be.

*Prying and intruding widens the gap.* Teenagers need privacy in which they can find themselves. They resent parents who pry as though they were not to be trusted. They rebel from too intrusive questioning. They want to receive their mail unopened. They like to know that their phone calls are not bugged. They need some secrets and secret places, not for wrongdoing, but just for being themselves. Parents recognizing their maturing children's rights for a modicum of privacy refrain from intruding. They await their children's approach to them out of respect for their growing sense of autonomy.

*No young person can be compared with any other.* Every individual is a unique human being, becoming more and more his own special kind of person. This is important to teenagers, especially. They may try to look like one another, but they resent being compared with others.

Parents know that it does not help to compare one child with any other. When you do, you lose the youngster you have been trying to impress. He turns from you and your implied criticism, because deep inside he knows he has to be himself. When you compare one of your children with another, you not only risk losing contact with him, but also of intensifying the sibling rivalry between the two.

You do well to point out each child's strengths and growing abilities, privately at times, and in the family circle occasionally. As each of your youngsters knows that he is respected for his own real talents and progress he is motivated far more powerfully than he ever could be by comparison with others.

*Being there when needed is important.* Many modern parents recognize how important it is to be available to their teenagers. They are needed now as much as they ever have been, but in different ways. What teenagers look for are opportunities to think through puzzling situations with parents who can be helpful without running off with the youngster's problem. This means being available both physically and emotionally.

Being emotionally reachable means a certain openness in your relationship. It implies your ability to look at a problem *with* your teenager and not have to use the situation to your own advantage. It requires your being interested, objective, and receptive.

*Learning to listen receptively* takes discipline. It is all too easy to listen with "half an ear" giving only partial attention to what is being told you. Louise's mother confesses that her daughter so prattles on and on that she finds her mind wandering to other things. Chester's father admits that it is hard for him to keep from "preaching" when young Chet opens up a controversial matter with him.

"You have to tune in to the music as well as to the words," observes a successful counselor of youth. He points out that it is how the youngster feels about what has happened and how he feels about himself that are most important in helping him take the next step that is right for him. No one else can live his life for him. He must find his own way, in his own time. When his parents sense where he is at the moment in his appraisal of himself, they have a chance of being available emotionally as well as in their physical presence.

## Maintaining Communication with Your Teens

There are a few basic principles of good communication that you can practice with your maturing youngsters. Of course you will get through to each of your children in ways that differ from your communication with any other. Your relationship with the same child now is not what it used to be. But, even with these inevitable differences, there are certain universals to keep in mind.

*Is anything discussable?* Families in which anyone can bring up any subject for discussion have an inside track with their teenagers. It is during the teen years that ideas and possibilities and attitudes are being explored. Today, especially, young people are considering all sorts of alternatives to the aspects of life they have known. Unflappable parents do not get shocked at their youngsters' way-out ideas. They can look at the questions their kids raise and the examples they cite as interesting without accepting or rejecting the implied proposals. This keeps the door open for family consideration in productive ways.

*What does it mean to you?* This is a key that opens many a locked door in the family. When you feel your inner temperature rising at what your teenager is saying, take a deep breath and ask as quietly as you can, "What does this mean to you, dear?" You may get an immediate, "Nothing at all, Mom, I was just wondering." You may hear your youngster with pleading in her eyes, say, "Please hear me out, this means a lot to me." Helping your teenager put into words what the values are in the situation gives both of you insight into yourselves, as well as each other.

*Asking the right questions* maintains communication. You are on safe ground when your teenager's disturbing report draws to a close, to ask softly, "How did you feel then?" This enables the youngster to look at his own reaction to the problem, and sort out his emotions about it. Your question has neither condemned nor condoned. It has merely attempted to put into focus the feelings inherent in the experience.

"What do you think can be done about it?" is another reliable way of raising a helpful question. The parent who hears his teenager's problem and immediately rushes in with a solution deprives his youngster of the chance to find his own way out of his dilemma. As suggestion after suggestion is made, your questioning may take the line, "And, what would that lead to?" thus helping your teenager evaluate the probable outcome of the several possible routes open to him. This does not imply that your judgment is to be ignored but that it is not introduced before your teenager is ready for it.

*Stating your own position clearly* at the right time. When your teenager comes to the place where he asks, "What do you think?" you have a responsibility to tell him as concisely as you can. Then you state your position, with reasons that are reasonable, and values that are explicit. When your own reaction is out of proportion to the facts of the case, you need not fear admitting why.

Debbie accused her father of raising his voice and yelling whenever his arguments were weak. He thought for a moment, and then acknowledged with a grin, "It's because I care so much for you that I cannot always be as cool as you might like me to be." Debbie's response was immediate. She hugged her dad in gratitude and the argument drew to a comfortable close for them both.

*Take time to be alone with your teenager.* Family togetherness can be stifling especially during the teen years. If through the years your children have been growing up, you have taken the time to be alone with each one at regular intervals, you have a foundation now for continuing communication. Now that bedtimes do not always synchronize as well as they did when you tucked your children in and heard their prayers at night, other one-to-one opportunities must be found.

When Sharon and her mother do the weekly shopping together they both look forward to the "girl talk" they share with one another. Sharon's mother has never laughed at her, but they do plenty of laughing with one another. They respect one another as persons, and it shows in the way they listen and respond to each other.

Alvin and his father are both outdoors men, and that gives them many happy hours together. One of their favorite games at such times is what they call, "devil's advocate." Then Alvin, or his father, takes a stance contrary to the other's just for the fun of seeing where it will lead. Alvin has learned in these sessions to respect his father's standards. His dad admires the way Alvin's mind works, and the clear way he can pursue an argument to its rational conclusion. Now, Alvin is considering going into law school, possibly because of the informal training in thinking clearly his father has encouraged.

There is no constant maturity for teenagers. Parents are not paragons of proficiency. Each generation matures as long as it lives. Each grows best in close interaction with others. This is a precious heritage as thinking, feeling creatures, who share a common time in history, under the guiding hand of the Father of us all.

# 16. LIVING WITH DIFFERENCES IN YOUR FAMILY

Your family was founded on difference as you and your spouse married. Husband and wife joined together with all the dissimilarities of their two sexes. Children came and differences between the generations emerged. Grandparents and other relatives add their dimension of difference to this day. No wonder that differences are considered normal in family life.

## Two or More Generations in the Family

You parents are caught in the middle of the conflict of generations. Your children arrive with few of your values built-in. They play havoc with you and your treasured possessions until you have taught them to respect persons and property. In time you have them trained, more or less, only to have them "spoiled" by an indulgent grandparent or childless aunt who keeps reminding you that "they are only children." If these older family members live with you, they are both a blessing and a problem at times, depending upon how well your personalities mesh.

*The generations see things differently,* because they grow up in different periods. Grandparents spent their childhood in the depression and war years when they learned to scrimp and save. To this day, many of them are shocked by the waste they see around them, as they cherish every scrap.

Your children, growing up in a period of plenty, relatively go to the opposite extreme. Their "throw it away and buy the new model" stance has been expected as they have been growing up. You keep after them to take care of their things, but the lessons of television commercials and the example of their friends are stiff competition.

*Styles differ with social change.* Clothing and grooming shifts in style are observable. What pleases one generation annoys another. What is expected by members of the older generation appears out-of-date to the younger members of the family. Their ways, on the other hand, upset their elders, who fuss about young people's hair styles, clothes and conduct.

In periods of rapid social change such as ours, generational differences are inevitable. Not only do members of the older, younger, and middle generations in the family behave differently, they feel differently, and they value different things. One of the big challenges of modern family life is learning to live with the differences harmoniously.

### Children in the Family Differ

No two children in the family are exactly alike. Each was born with his own set of genes and chromosomes that are uniquely his or hers. Even identical twins have some differences that their parents learn to recognize. All other children in the family can be expected to be different from the beginning. The older they grow the more they become themselves.

*Some sibling rivalry is to be expected.* Each child must find his or her own identity as different from all the others. Each must discover the ways in which he is stronger, brighter, more talented, or more favored, if he can. Try as hard as you will, you cannot ever divide yourself equally among your children. From time to time one may feel left out, in disgrace, or discriminated against, even in the fairest of families. This aggravates the squabbling that most parents find distressing.

*Children's differences tend to be loud.* You may try to ignore your children's quarrels as long as you can. But you find yourself interfering to protect the weaker ones, and to keep a little peace and quiet in the house. Studies find that when parents try to find "who started it" or who is to blame for the children's fuss, the squabbling only becomes more frequent and lasting. With wise supervision, children resolve their own differences, most of the time.

*Helping each child feel good about himself* is the most effective approach to reducing brother-sister quarrelling. As you give special one-to-one attention to each of your children, in ways that are clear and reassuring, the children do not have to compete for the recognition they all need. Your example in times of stress serves as a model for your children. You can hear yourself as your youngsters ape your tone of voice, words, and behavior. When you feel good, the children behave. When you are out

rts, the youngsters reflect your mood then too. This is one
n why it is important for parents to avoid as much tension
ey can.

## Husband-Wife Differences

Differences between husband and wife are normal in most marriages. Two people who intimately share everything they have (and are) are bound to run into some conflict from time to time. A good marriage is not necessarily one in which the pair see eye to eye on everything all the time. Rather it is one in which they both understand their differences and attempt to work them out harmoniously.

*Changing roles of men and women* cause problems in marriage. Now when nine out of ten women work at some time in their marriage, both husbands and wives attempt to develop new ways of interaction than they once knew. Most young husbands now feel that they should help their wives in the busiest part of the family day. The man returns to find his wife trying to prepare the evening meal while keeping the tired, hungry children amused. So, he takes the youngsters off for a playtime, or a bath and story so that supper can be readied in peace. That is all very well. But, many a man does not yet feel at home in the household. And, there are women contented who prefer to do themselves the things they learned as girls were women's work.

When the wife feels put upon in carrying more than her share of the responsibility, she becomes sulky. When the husband tries to help without the required skills, his bungling efforts can be annoying. Because both are trying roles they did not learn as children, they are awkward and ill at ease. The problem is compounded when one or both of the pair have not thought through what they have a right to expect of each other and of themselves.

*Off days come to everyone.* In marriage they are a peculiar challenge. A young husband gets used to seeing his wife out of sorts the days before she menstruates. Her husband discovers that it is wise not to ruffle her overmuch just before her period each month. The wife often is uncomfortable during the first three months and the last part of her pregnancy. She is tired after giving birth, and then gets the blues soon after she and the baby return home from the hospital. These downs and ups in female rhythm have to be lived with in any marriage.

A man can become dog-tired at the end of his working day. Then he needs comforting and building up instead of the accumulated troubles of the household as soon as he steps inside the door. He gets discouraged at times, and his wife would like to cheer him up if she can. They both need to feel the other's love, in the way they want it at the moment. Unfortunately their moods do not always synchronize.

*Husband and wife define their most intimate moments* differently. When they have had a falling out, he tends to feel, "If she would just let me love her up a little, everything would be all right again." But, his wife's reaction is, "Don't you come near me until you have apologized and made things right again." He sees lovemaking as a balm; she views it as a reward for good behavior. Until they get their philosophy of intimacy in accord, they will have some unhappy times. Fortunately, many a couple now get premarital counseling, and go for marital consultation before the problem becomes too critical.

*Because you care, your differences hurt.* Someone else whom you know only casually can say something that would cut deeply coming from someone you love. It is our nearest and dearest who wound us most often. Members of the family know where we are vulnerable. Lovers and mates have ways of intruding upon the inner citadel each tries to protect from attack. So lovers' quarrels and marital conflicts arise from time to time among pairs who care for one another.

### Can Conflict Be Constructive?

"There's nothing like a good fight to clear the air at our house," says a father we know. He goes on to say that when his wife gets moody he knows that a storm is brewing between them. Some little thing trips them off, and she lets him know what it is that has been bothering her. In the heat of the marital spat, he gets things off his chest that he has been bottling up. They fight it out, and feel better for clearing the issues that have upset them both.

*You say things in anger* that you would not dare express otherwise. This has both positive and negative results. It is helpful to express genuine feelings so that both you and your partner understand how you feel. But it can hurt you both when accusations are made that undermine your confidence in yourselves, in one another and in your marriage.

*How to fight fair is learned* in action. The child who has never seen his parents express their differences, grows up with little or no experience in the techniques of creative conflict. Parents who openly disagree from time to time, let their children know that differences are to be expected, and that they can be worked through without harm.

Constructive quarreling is based upon two fundamental rules. One, attack the issues rather than each other. Two, state your case, clearly without attempting to analyze or accuse the other person. When your conflict focusses on the issue that separates you, ways can be found around it. Accusing your partner only irks him further, and does nothing to resolve the problem. Each of you needs to understand how the situation looks from your own point of view. You owe it to one another to put your case as clearly and concisely as you can.

*Making up is so pleasant* that a neglected wife may pick a fight with her husband for the satisfaction of having his un-divided attention for awhile. This is risky business. If repeated too often, he learns to avoid her even more. But, it is true that after a conflict has been resolved there is a sweet period of coming together that unifies a couple. They feel closer than ever after they have worked through a difficult problem, successfully. They have a security of knowing, "If we can live through that, we can take anything that happens to us!"

## Two Rocky Roads to Avoid

Throughout history men and women have used two methods of resolving their differences that have proven themselves too harmful to continue. Learning to live with differences in your family involves unlearning both of these. You probably picked up one or both habits as a child. Now, before these become established as permanent parts of your personalities, you can help each other discard them.

*Open warfare is dangerous,* at home and abroad. Fighting it out settles nothing, and only widens the breach. People get hurt, often seriously in the chronic warfare that goes on in some homes. The assumption is that the one who wins a battle is right while he who loses must have been wrong. It is never that simple. In fact, marshalling ammunition and "letting the other have it" is acting out the might-makes-right fallacy. Religious people rightly recoil from this philosophy, and try to resolve their differences amicably.

*Pretending the problem does not exist* is harmful for another reason. When you act as though you are not upset when you really are, you ignore your angry feelings. But ignoring them does not make them go away. They are there more powerful than ever because they have been driven underground.

Repressing anger is like swallowing a corrosive substance. It eats at you from inside, literally. Medicine is replete with cases of good people who give themselves chronic headaches, ulcers, and other psychosomatic ailments by habitually swallowing their emotions.

## Ten Steps to Peace in the Family

Peace does not come in a single step, but in a pathway that leads to harmony. Nothing is more important in relationships with others than mastering the elements of peacemaking. You can begin now to perfect your approaches to peaceful living in your family. You start with yourself, and in time the others follow your lead. Some of these ten steps you find easy, others more difficult. They all are worth your time and effort, now and for the future of your family.

(1) *Accept the fact of difference.* Differences are inevitable in the intimate interaction of free persons. Do not waste time blaming others for your problems. Self-pity is quite self-destructive. The way out is through honest recognition of the differences that have arisen between you and others in the family.

(2) *Face each problem as it arises.* Ask yourself, "What is the trouble here?" Try to sense how you really feel about it. When you and the person with whom the difficulty has come up are alone, calmly suggest that you look together for its resolution. Express your loving concern as you suggest the problem be tackled. Then quietly listen to the others' response.

(3) *Look for the causes of the conflict.* Ask yourselves, "When did the problem first arise?" "What has been happening between us?" "What brought about our current hassle?" These are not academic questions, for which ready answers are possible. They require soul-searching as well as hard work for both of you.

(4) *Put your goals and values into words.* Ask yourself: "What am I after in this struggle? What does it matter to me? Why am I so upset about it?" You may find that your reaction is

unnecessarily intense. Something is upsetting you unduly about a matter that actually is too trivial to make an issue over. Or, you may discover that a basic principle is involved that is worth preserving.

(5) *Appraise the outcome of this problem.* "Where are we headed?" is the question. Watch that you not become melodramatic about what lies ahead for you and your relationship. Consider to what extent you can continue to live with the difference that bothers you now. Suppose the other person does not change, can you do the adapting? Are you willing and able to live within your situation indefinitely?

(6) *Empathize with the other person.* Try to get the feel of what he or she is going through. Attempt to put yourself in the other's shoes as much as you can. Ask kindly, "What does this mean to you, honey?" Then, sensitively listen to the other's responses and reaction. Do not assume that you can read him like a book. Realize that you can never know another human being completely, but that you can increase your understanding of him and of yourself, if you earnestly try.

(7) *Consider your alternatives.* Think through what might be done to solve the problem. Beware of generalizing, "If only you would . . . " Talk over instead what you both might do as the next step in your efforts to please one another. Brainstorm what possibilities there are for you both. Keep your mood as lighthearted as possible so that you can laugh together at the more ridiculous suggestions. Humor releases tension, so that you both can think more clearly.

(8) *Make a plan of action* that is acceptable to everyone. Determine together who will do what and how in the proposed program of action. Make sure that each person gets a real chance to suggest what he will do to help rather than be told by some dominant member of the team. Proceed at a leisurely pace so that the youngest and weakest may have time to mobilize their resources and make a contribution to the discussion.

(9) *Get to know yourself and each other* in your problem-solving approaches. Sense how each of you usually responds to confrontation with a new problem. Use the resolution of your conflicts as opportunities for deeper understanding of one another. In the process of peacekeeping withdraw in meditation and prayer for the guidance you need.

(10) *Live for joint purposes beyond yourselves.* Families who

live for causes greater than themselves have fewer difficulties than do self-centered homes. Persons whose concerns are beyond the moment have little time for petty squabbles. This may be why service-oriented persons have happier families than do those who live for material things alone. Ministers, teachers, and social workers who give themselves to helping others have statistically happier marriages than do those who use others exploitively.

## Families Are Laboratories of Peace

International conferences warrant the headlines in news releases. But peace in the world is being made not only at conference tables where heads of state gather. "Since wars begin in the hearts of men" is axiomatic. Peace in the world is homemade wherever persons learn to live with their differences in harmony.

*Kitchen table conferences* set the stage for peacemaking on a larger scale. As father, mother and children gather together to nourish their bodies and minds and spirits, they work at the very heart of lasting peacemaking. They work through each perplexing daily difference that arises. They are not afraid of confrontation or consultation. Their experience in facing life together and with courage is rewarding. They trust themselves and they have confidence in one another out of their practice of peace in their own home.

# 17. AVOIDING TENSION BUILD-UP

There are many tense moments in the lives of modern parents. Parents are under pressure while their babies are small, and they get even more tired when the children are toddlers. School-agers give parents little time to themselves. So, learn to reduce your tensions as much as you can as you go along.

Conscientious parents are especially vulnerable, because they try so hard to do what is right for their children. The harder you try the more tension builds up. You do not want to be so relaxed that you become irresponsible and slovenly. But perhaps you could reduce the stress in the family that comes from your tension.

## Tense Parents—Uneasy Families

*Tension runs through families.* You can feel it like an electric charge as soon as you set foot in the door. Father comes in, sees that his wife is uneasy, and reacts by being disagreeable himself. She turns and dashes to the kitchen, tripping over her son's skate en route. He gets a cuff on the ear, and chases the dog outside. The dog chases the cat, who howls all night from the back fence. Something like this happens from time to time in any family in which tension is allowed to build up.

*Children reflect the mood of their parents.* Both now and in later life, children respond to their parents' emotional climate as they do to changes in the weather. When purr words predominate, everyone feels at ease, and things go smoothly. When slur words fall like hail, the family members learn to protect themselves as best they can. The best defense is not always a strong offense. But it is frequently tried by children too young to know better. Before anyone knows what is happening there is a house-ful of tense, unhappy people.

*Unhappy baggage from childhood* plagues many people. Harry

.disliked his father's grumbling as a lad, but he finds himself doing the same thing now as a parent. Gertrude always felt sad when her mother complained. But now a woman grown, she uses the same minor key and words she heard her mother whine when she was but a girl. Children absorb their parents' poor habits, as well as their nicer traits. Unfortunately, these moods learned in childhood are hard to shake off. If you want to break the vicious cycle before your children pick up the ways that have made life difficult for you, this chapter is for you.

## Marriage Blowups over Little Things

You know how marital squabbles come over trivial things, not worth fussing about. In the face of a real crisis, you pull together as a real team. But from time to time you have a terrific blowup and when it is all over you ask yourselves in dismay, "What was *that* all about?" The chances are that it came when one or both of you had let tension build up to the explosive point.

*Controlling your temper is not enough.* You may vow on your knees to hold your tongue from now on, and not lose your patience with your loved ones. But there is a next time and the time after that. It is not a matter of willing your discomfort away. You have to avoid the reason for being distraught in the first place. This means understanding yourself and the others in the family well enough to spot signs of tension build up before it goes too far.

*Indications that you need a change of pace* are numerous. You wake up tired after a restless night. Something is bothering you and you can't be sure what it is. Your step has lost its spring, your voice its lilt. You feel out of sorts, depressed, and edgy. Unless you tip off your mate that you are under the weather, he is apt to feel that he has done something to displease you. That makes him feel guilty without knowing why. You see your distress mirrored in his face, and you feel ashamed. But by this time you are too upset to tell him so. So, the uneasiness grips you both until he leaves for the day.

*Alert your dear ones that you are not up to par,* and the clouds scatter. Your partner no longer feels guilty. He and the children do what they can to make you feel better. It does help, and you are able to mobilize yourself to send them off without feeling too sorry for you. Over the hump of your blues, you plan a treat for these dear ones of yours, and the day is saved. The magic comes from admitting the problem is within yourself, so the blame won't have to be fixed on someone else.

## Maintaining Your Marriage

Christian parents often err in putting their children first in their lives. They work so hard for their youngsters that they have little or no time for themselves. Worse yet, their marriage suffers from neglect. The happiness they should be finding in one another eludes them. They become tense and uneasy. Then they need to see their marriage as of primary importance for the well-being of their children, their family, and themselves.

*Your mate comes first.* Take a recognizable example. He comes home disappointed at the way his day went. She sees the sag in his shoulders before he says a word. She knows he needs her now, more than the children do. So, she calls her mother, or a reliable sitter, and readies herself to be available to her husband exclusively for awhile. After they have had a quiet hour or two together they share a new lease on life and a new faith in their marriage. The children gather around secure in their parents' love. They sense that their mother is not at their beck and call always, but that she and their father have something special going for them.

*You are not too old for fun and games.* Being able to play is not a matter of chronological age. If you and your spouse can have fun together—good old-fashioned playfulness—you have a lot going for you. Parenthood becomes burdensome when the merriment goes out of it. Life becomes too deadly serious, too heavy to bear. The answer is in having fun as you go along. Try being lighthearted and amusing when you come together at the end of the day. Whisper nonsense into your lover's ear. Remember to share the funny things that happen during the day. Enter into your children's fun. They can teach you to let go and enjoy life, if you let them. You parents need to play quite as much as your children do. You'll love it, and they will love you for it.

*Build one another up.* Nothing nourishes a marriage like mutual admiration. Tell your sweetheart how smart, handsome, lithe, and wonderful he is. Let your wife know that you adore the way she walks and that she is as attractive to you now as on the day you met. She may accuse you of being silly, but she needs to hear such compliments from you. You each have to know that you are loved and lovable, if your marriage is to keep on being sweet and good. You discover the meaning of love with one another, in day by day soothing as well as nocturnal stroking.

## You Do Not Have to be Perfect

Never being satisfied is hard on you and on the others who live with you. It is all very well to have high standards, but not so high that you bruise yourself against them.

*Striving for perfection is hard on you.* It keeps you discontented with yourself, and dissatisfied with life. It is difficult for your mate and your children. No matter how hard they try, they cannot be sure of pleasing you if you keep pushing them to excel beyond their strength. If God had wanted you to be an angel, he would not have made you human. So, relax in your humanness and enjoy it. It will help you avoid tension build up.

*Letting things go* will not be the end of the world. It is presumptuous of you to assume that you have to carry everything on your shoulders. Your place in life is to do what you can without strain. Pushing yourself beyond what you easily can do makes you tense. It disrupts your family, and turns off your friends.

## Can It Wait Till Later?

Have you ever found yourself pushing to finish something that might wait? You get into a project and get so absorbed that you lose all track of time. You are so eager to complete it, before you take care of the children, or get a meal, that you find yourself working under pressure? This is one of the ways that tension builds up.

*The completion complex is costly.* Attempting to finish off a job before tackling your next daily routine exacts a heavy price at times. You find yourself with a throbbing head, and other physical signs of stress when you get yourself into the completion complex. What is the completion complex? It is the irrational attempt to finish a job that does not necessarily have to be completed immediately. It not only is unnecessary, it exacts a heavy toll in emotional well-being.

*People can't wait, things can.* A child is his present age only once. His needs must be met now or not at all. This does not mean that you have to drop everything the minute your child calls. But it does imply that anything else can wait: the cleaning, the bed-making, the project of the moment. But your time with your youngsters is a precious once-only experience now. This goes double for your relationship with your husband. When he needs you he has a right to you; and you have the privilege of attending him as though nothing else matters. A grand lady I know puts it, "I'm the only wife my husband has, and I want to keep it that way!"

*Keep routines simple.* One of the things you learn through experience is to simplify your routines. As you slip out of bed in the morning, pull the bedding straight and you save yourself the bed-making chore later. Dishes dry well in the drainer after a hot rinse and you save the time of wiping them. Stacking soiled dishes in the washer and running it once a day saves time and helps the ecology. A jar of peanut butter on the table enables you to fix each youngsters snack as he wants it and saves the time of making sandwiches ahead. A myriad of other shortcuts are possible in any family. Heloise has built a large clientele by hints for homemakers to which you can add your own as you discover shortcuts.

## Being Good to Come Home To

You are an important part of your family. If you let yourself get overly tired, when you feel put-upon and overworked, you are not your best self. You owe it to your family to keep yourself feeling fit, satisfied, and happy. How do you do that? By meeting your own needs as you go along.

*Take a break when you can.* Workers in factory or office get regular breaks morning and afternoon. You who make your own schedule as a homemaker are entitled to no less. When the baby naps, give yourself a break and do what most relaxes you. When the children leave for school, catch your own breath before plunging into the things that must be done. Before the family comes together in the late afternoon, snatch a few minutes to shower, comb your hair, and relax. Even in the midst of a crisis, with a sick child or a long wait in the hospital, break your vigil with a walk down the corridor, or sit loose and breathe deeply a few times to relax the tension.

*Get the rest you need.* Parents are the most overworked people in town. They are on call twenty-four hours a day, day and night, week after week. Responsibilities assumed by father and mother in supporting and caring for the family are gladly undertaken, but heavy nevertheless. If you parents are to be good to live with, you must get the rest you need, when you need it. There will be some evenings when you want to tumble into bed as soon as the children—do it. Nap or take it easy for fifteen or twenty minutes after your noon and evening meals and you'll be amazed at how refreshed you feel. Learn to let go when you can. Fall asleep in the midst of a television program without feeling guilty. Tired children are cranky; so are parents.

*Keep personal interests alive.* Nothing is so frustrating as feeling that you can't do what you would like to do if you could. Mothers are apt to be trapped into their daily schedules at home. They get discouraged about their own growth and development. This is a mistake. If you have always wanted to learn to play the organ, don't pressure your kids into music lessons; take them yourself—now. Set aside an hour a day for what you like doing. If you enjoy painting, paint. If writing is your forte, write. If there is a class in adult education you would enjoy, arrange your schedule so that you can take it. You'll be a happier person for not depriving yourself of the personal enrichment that makes you glad to be you.

*Husbands and wives are interchangeable* as parents. Mother plays catch with her son when father has a golf date Saturday afternoon. Father cares for the household the evening mother's course comes. Mother does the laundry while father mops the kitchen floor; and they both team up in settling the youngsters down at night. Sharing work is more fun, and it releases time for personal interests you both like to keep alive.

*You are more interesting companions* when you keep on your toes. Cartoonists have a field day portraying parties where the women cluster discussing their children, and the men separate to talk about sports. This is too true to life to be funny. It does not have to be that way.

## Single Parents' Special Pressures

You may be a single parent; if not you know one or more. Raising children alone is not unusual today. A divorce or separation, the death of the spouse, a prolonged absence from the family for whatever reason puts the burden for child-rearing on the remaining parent.

*One parent instead of two.* Mothers without husbands have to try to be both for their children. Their mother roles are fairly easy, because they are familiar. But, trying to be a father too is difficult. Fathers have a special role in the lives of their daughters (to give them a living example of what a man is, and how to relate to him). They are important for their son's development in serving as the model of manhood he follows.

Fathers as single parents are in a double bind. They have to mother their children as well as be fathers; and they act counter to ways in which men are supposed to behave. One lone father we know says it annoys him to have the women on his street clucking their sympathy for him as he shops with his children; drops off their soiled clothing at the launderette; or attends other parental duties normally assigned a wife. He says that the kids and he do all right, if only the neighbors would let them alone!

*Relatives and neighbors play special roles.* There is nothing like a nearby grandfather who enjoys taking a fatherless boy to a ball game, or helping him fix his bike. The woman who picks up the girl whose mother is no longer at home, for a cookie-baking party is serving a real need.

Finding substitute-parents for absent ones is central in movements like the Big Brothers, Big Sisters, Foster Grandparents, and other organizations designed to fill gaps left by parents. These programs give neighbors a chance to enjoy children in their lives while giving the youngsters the benefit of their time and attention.

*Single parents need adult companionship.* Two parents sharing their childbearing interests talk over the daily occurrences that please or perplex them. They look forward to their time with each other as mutually rewarding. Such easy access is wanting in the single parent family, unless some special effort is made to provide it.

There may be a Parents Without Partners group in your community. This program brings together men and women who are raising children unaided by a second parent. In their meetings they discuss their children; and they provide the adult companionship that most single parents need from time to time. Do not be afraid that such an organization is primarily a matchmaking operation. At least look into it, if yours is a single parent home.

*Find a trustworthy confidante.* This can be a respected neighbor or friend. It may be your pastor, or doctor, or a counselor at your local guidance service. It should be someone with whom you can talk over the things that bother you as they arise. Letting them pile up until you can no longer think clearly about them makes you anxious. It prevents you from being the relaxed and stable parent your children need. Every human being needs to have someone with whom he or she can be himself. Often that one special person is a husband or wife. Single parents must develop this close contact with some other adult who is both accessible and understanding.

*Spare your children your loneliness.* No child should bear the full burden of a parent's anguish. As a single mother or father, you have your problems, sure. Some of these can be shared with your children as part of the team in the family. But your loneliness, your sense of being bereft, your urgent need to reveal yourself to another at times, is for another adult, not your children.

## Reducing Tension

Everyone must find ways of being nice to live with. Tempers have to be controlled, and blue moods kept to a minimum for good family living. You have your own ways of reducing tension and maintaining your well-being. Think about the following suggestions that have worked well for others; they may be helpful to you, too.

*Alternate your tasks* to keep from overtaxing yourself in any one. After a hard physical chore, take on some sedentary job next to give yourself a change in pace. Tackle the unpleasant things that have to be done when you are feeling fit and follow them up with things you especially enjoy doing. Give yourself a little treat when you have completed an especially demanding project. This gives you something to look forward to while you are working. Anticipated rewards keep you going better than the inner scolding that tightens you in tension.

*Get things done at your own rate.* You have ways of doing things that make them easier for you than pushing yourself too fast or dragging yourself along at a snail's pace. If you are working beside a whirlwind, do not let the other's pace upset you; keep to the rhythm that suits you best. Before you become irritable, change the pace of your activity and do something else for awhile. Then you can come back to the difficult situation when you have a fresh perspective on it.

*Make a family project of complicated jobs.* Many hands make light work, and are fun when everyone pitches in. Housecleaning time can be shared with the members of the family by listing the things to be done, and having each person volunteer to do the thing he or she is willing to tackle. Polishing the silver, cleaning the basement, putting in a garden, freezing and preserving, all can be tiring and tension-producing alone, but easier and more pleasant when everyone shares the load.

*Express your feelings,* and talk out your troubles. Your bottled up feelings give you tension fatigue quicker than the hardest physical work. The principle to follow is to acknowledge the emotion that stirs you and express it in constructive ways. Love and tenderness flow easily within the family. Anger, jealousy, and feeling rejected or put upon are harder to express. These negative feelings build up tension within you unless you release them.

Talk out your problems without making others feel guilty about them. This is especially important in family life. You spread your anxiety throughout the family when you make the others feel that it was their fault that you feel so bad. You have to learn to share your problems in ways that allow others to help you get the strength you need.

Prayer helps you get perspective as you share your worries with the Power beyond yourself. You rise in a few minutes feeling better for having a broader view of the problem. Making a regular practice of meditating as you start your day gives you calmness and strength for whatever happens.

*Learn to be flexible.* Rigidity is hard on you and those you live with. The person who can see only one right way to do or be, tightens up and tries to defend himself rather than bending with the burden. Living with other persons in the intimacy of your home calls for listening well to the ideas and suggestions of the other members of the family. When you can honestly say, "You may be right," or "Let's try it your way," you give others a chance to assume responsibility; and you keep yourself from getting uptight about some approach that may not be worth the struggle.

Relax, and enjoy each day as it comes, and your loved ones will find you nice to come home to.

# 18. FAMILY TIES—TO MAN AND GOD

"We never were a close family," said the woman sadly. She sat all alone in what might have been a hotel room anywhere in the world. Why are some families so cold and unhappy, and others so warm and close?

## Secrets of Happy Families

Hundreds of thousands of happy families have been studied in recent years to find out what makes for happiness in family life. Not all the mystery has been unravelled, but a few factors are crystal clear.

*Sharing similar interests helps.* Family ties are forged by members who enjoy doing things together. They have enough common interests and talents to become involved with one another.

*Freedom for each to be oneself is important.* Francis was born into a family of intellectuals. His father was a Latin scholar; his mother was a student of Greek. But Francis' inclination from the beginning was in physical activity. He had a sturdy body that called for exercise. His talents were in gymnastics to which he devoted hours every day from the time he was not quite six. Fortunately his parents encouraged his talent for athletic activity and lived to see him a state finalist. More important than the name he made for himself in athletics was the feeling of mutual appreciation he and his parents had forged.

*Spiritual values in action* make for family strength. Material values are all right in their place, but they encourage competition, competitiveness, and greed. Spiritual values in contrast are sharable. One way to view spiritual values is that they are increased by sharing. Examples are love, friendship, mutual support and encouragement, knowledge, faith, and commitment. All these values are developed in interaction. They grow best in a climate of mutual sharing.

*Enjoying one another in the family* is an essential element. Close family ties begin with husband and wife, and parents and children who enjoy one another. The pleasure of being together comes from liking one another sincerely. It is not enough to say you love your children. You have to *like* them and let them know it to weave the closeness they and you need. This begins early and continues as long as the family lasts.

### Relax and Enjoy Your Little Children

Tiny tots are fascinating little people. They are full of life and the zest for living. They make every minute count, and know how to bring every bit of sweetness to the fore. Enter this kingdom "as a little child" and you find yourself surrounded by magic, and surfeited with mystery.

*Curiosity and imagination* are delightful in little ones. Anything can be explored and investigated with enthusiasm. You can be too busy to listen to your youngster's endless questions; or you can look at them as he does, and get a whole new perspective on what has become commonplace.

*Affection-needing and love-giving* warm your heart. Gretchen backs up to her father with the smiling demand, "make a lap," into which she cuddles contentedly. George dashes to his mother for a good-bye kiss when he leaves and gives her a pat when he returns. Each in his own way show their need for affection and their fullhearted giving of love. How chilly your life would be without this warmth!

*Rituals start early.* Most little children love to do things the way they have always done them. They especially enjoy the rituals of your family. Little heads bow at table in families where grace at meals is expected. Loud amens in treble keys cap any blessing or prayer. Stories have to be read in the same way, time after time. Skip a few pages, and your four-year-old objects.

### Older Children as Good Companions

Your happiest times may be those when you have a house full of children. These are the busy years when life bubbles around you with the enthusiasms of childhood. There probably is too little time, or space, or money for everything you would like to have for them. But they already have the best of gifts—you.

*Sharing insights and information* highlight homes with children. The youngsters come trooping in full of their day's experiences, eager for a chance to regale you with them. If you are not too busy to listen, you will get an earful. You enter into the kingdom of the young-at-heart as you see things with their eyes and begin to feel with them. You learn a great deal about school, and other children and their families, and how life looks to your son or daughter.

The way you react to your child's accounts determines how much he continues to tell you. Cut him off with a remonstrance, and you risk losing his further confidences. Listen closely, and you encourage him to come to you. Comment when he asks you to, as candidly and kindly as you can, and you share a precious bond of communication.

*Pitching in to get jobs* done cements a sense of family. From daily chores to weekly shopping and on to the big projects of the season, your children add a great deal. They love to help, if you start them early and make them feel a real part of the family. They often surprise you with their resourcefulness. You are proud of the way they assume responsibility. Underneath is the sense of family you all get from working together at the tasks at hand.

*Keeping you young* is an unexpected boon. You have always loved your children. When they were babies, you enjoyed caring for them most of the time. Now you find that your children keep you youthful in many ways. Doing things with them gives you the exercise you need that your childless friends have to purposely take on as a chore. Living with children makes you young at heart, if you are not too heavy-handed an adult.

### Teenagers Stretch Your Mind (and Patience)

Recent studies of teenagers' values give you an inkling of what they, and you, are going through. Today's young people are found to value human dignity, to search for sanctity in all of life, and to want more meaning as human beings. These are sacred values deeply rooted in Christianity. You cannot quarrel with teenagers' goals. The ways they take in pursuit of these age-old ideals you may find disturbing.

*Modern youth wants to be relevant.* By this they mean to be at one with nature, to put high value on sensory experience, and to emphasize being rather than doing. Their clothing and hair styles may be casual to extremes you find upsetting. Their rejection of anything artificial or phoney disturbs your sense of order and authority.

*Life's major questions surface* in the teen years. Together you face the role of education in life and in career planning. Decisions are being made now about friendships, social life, love affairs, and the many steps that lead to (or away from) marriage. The big issue of the kind of person one's teenager wants to become hits you and him with full force. His whole future depends upon his sense of who he is becoming; your years of caring for him are intricately woven into what he has become to date.

*Character is built in many moods.* To hear some people talk you would think that solemnity is necessary for morality. Not so. There are solemn occasions, of course, in any family, in every life. But many days are filled with laughter and good humor. Who is to say that the rain is better than the sun for a garden? It takes both to grow a rose or a noble character.

Being able to laugh at oneself is a precious heritage you can share with your children. It involves a willingness to be wrong, to be human, to be less than perfect. It saves the situation in many a family when feelings run high and dissension is imminent. Many a teenager has taught this knack to his or her parents. The grunt of recognition. "Here we go again" relieves the tension and makes communication possible. Key words that trigger a family memory have a saving grace when the going gets rough. Your youngster may sound impertinent, but listen, he may be saying something that eases the strain on the whole family. After all, he has known you all his life, and has learned more than he knows under your roof.

## Young Adult Sons and Daughters

Comes the time in every family when the children have grown and gone. This leaves you parents in "the empty nest" or does it? Chances are the young adults come flocking home for the holidays, to leave the children with you for awhile, to vacation with you, and to get your help with their major problems and projects.

*Caring continues* long after children are grown. They will be your children as long as you live. If you are not too possessive about them, they enjoy you and your ongoing affection. You have to mature along with your young adult children. You have to be grown up enough to let them live their own lives without interference. You have to be resourceful enough to fill your days with interest so that they won't feel guilty at leaving you. You take in your daughters-in-law and your sons-in-law with just the right amount of interest. Too much and they shy off; too little and they feel you don't care. Soon there are grandchildren for you and a whole new dimension comes into your life.

## Grandparents Give a Dimension in Depth

Grandparents are special people in the lives of most families. They are there when they are needed.

*A sense of history and continuity* is a contribution of older members of a family. Your children probably urge their grandparents to tell them about "the olden days when you were young." They like to hear about what their mothers and fathers were like when they were children. They get a sense of continuity within the family as they hear about ancestors they never met. A feeling of family pride helps a child develop his own identity as a person of worth. Knowing of the amusing and foolish things members of the family have done, gives you all an assurance that people are not perfect, but can be enjoyed and loved nevertheless.

*Parents are the bridge between the generations.* You find yourself in the middle between the requests of your children on the one hand and your parents on the other. As the middle generation, you form the bridge between the others. Your appreciation of your children helps your parents better understand youth. Your respect for older family members sets an example for your children. When all members of the family feel that they are cherished as very special people, something fine happens in the spirit of the family.

## Every Age Has Its Appeal

Every stage of life is filled with wonder. There is no period in the life cycle that can be called dull or uninteresting. As long as an individual keeps on growing, he experiences the unique satisfactions of his stage of life.

*Children grow up so fast!* You have to keep on your toes not to miss the wonder of every stage of a child's growth. You must relax and keep open to your youngsters to catch the nuances of their development. Your eyes and ears and arms are kept wide so as not to miss the novelty they bring to you. Be away even for a few days and you find you have missed something special in their maturing.

*The rich, full years are hectic.* When your home is bursting with noise and toys, clutter and children, you feel that you may not last to see the children grown. You fall into bed soon after the youngsters, as tired as they from the busy day. Your older sister comes for a visit and reminds you that these are your "rich full years." But, at the moment you would settle for an hour or two of peace and quiet. Time passes, the children grow up and leave home, and you are left with your memories of how wonderful everything was during those earlier days. You even miss the peanut butter kisses, the banged knees, and bruised egos that go with growing up. You know now your sister was right. Your challenge now is to fill your later years with the beauty and wisdom your children brought you.

*When the children are grown,* you find new challenges. For the first time in your life you are free to do what *you* want to do. While you were growing up, you did what your parents and teachers expected of you. You married and tried to please your life partner. The children came and you were at their beck and call. Now, your life is yours to live as you will. You can throw yourself into community service, devote yourself to church work, or prepare yourself for a second career ahead. Many men and women are doing just that these days. Now when more persons live their full life span in better health than did their parents they have the time, energy, and interest to give fully of themselves as long as they live.

### Ties to the Eternal

Your family ties are to one another, of course. But, fine as these relationships are, they are flat. Your present contacts give you a horizontal life with no height or depth unless you stretch upward and outward in your daily living.

*The vertical dimension of your life* appears as you tie in to the eternal. You and your family acknowledge your faith, as you reach upward together. You worship the same God, and pray similar prayers as you stretch up beyond yourselves. You and your children seem a generation apart until you see yourselves all as children of God, when your ages are of little importance. Viewing your lives as the heavenly Father would see them makes you search the depth of your being. Sham and pretense are impossible when you stand open and exposed to the light of his presence. You see yourself as you really are. You know you need help to be what you should be. You find amazing grace close by as you come one by one to find the Lord.

*Your greatest joy is in leading your children* to the good life that you have found in your ties to the eternal. They each go their own way as they grow up, but they can never cut off the rootage you gave them in a devout Christian family experience. Your faith encourages them to believe. Your commitment inspires them to give themselves to causes beyond the moment. Your concern for others sends them out into the world with compassion and sensitivity. In time, they return to you with the depth of their experience that enlarges your own.

*Becoming is better than having.* This is one of the most important lessons you and your children can learn in this day and age. You are surrounded by families who spend their time amassing quantities of things for themselves, their homes, and their leisure life. You can lay waste your powers trying to keep up with the Joneses. Or, you can take a noncompetitive stance and give yourself to higher values.

Your tie to the eternal gives you the vision you need. Your children are the better for trying to become worthy persons. You find your life as you lose it in purposes larger than you are—as you were told many centuries ago. You find one another as you tie in to the eternal.

# INDEX